TOP **10**

MAUI

MOLOKA'I & LANA'I

BONNIE FRIEDMAN

EYEWITNESS TRAVEL

Left **Ka'ahumanu Church** Center **Sugar Cane Train, Lahaina** Right **Napili Bay**

LONDON, NEW YORK,
MELBOURNE, MUNICH AND DELHI
www.dk.com

Produced by Blue Island, London
Reproduced by Colourscan, Singapore
Printed and bound by South China
Printing Co. Ltd, China
First American Edition, 2004
10 11 12 13 10 9 8 7 6 5 4 3 2 1

Published in the United States by
DK Publishing, 375 Hudson Street,
New York, New York 10014

**Reprinted with revisions 2006, 2008, 2010
Copyright 2004, 2010 ©
Dorling Kindersley Limited, London
A Penguin Company**

Published in Great Britain by
Dorling Kindersley Limited.

A catalog record for this book is available
from the Library of Congress.

ISSN 1479-344X
ISBN 978-0-75666-086-4

Within each Top 10 list in this book, no hierarchy of
quality or popularity is implied. All 10 are, in the
editor's opinion, of roughly equal merit.

Contents

Maui's Top 10

The information in this DK Eyewitness Top 10 Travel Guide is checked regularly.
Every effort has been made to ensure that this book is as up-to-date as possible at the time of
going to press. Some details, however, such as telephone numbers, opening hours, prices,
gallery hanging arrangements, and travel information are liable to change. The publishers
cannot accept responsibility for any consequences arising from the use of this book, nor for
any material on third party websites, and cannot guarantee that any website address in this
book will be a suitable source of travel information. We value the views and suggestions of
our readers very highly. Please write to: Publisher, DK Eyewitness Travel Guides,
Dorling Kindersley, 80 Strand, London, Great Britain WC2R 0RL.

Left **Windsurfing, Ho'okipa** Center **Ruby's Dinner, Kahului** Right **Keka'a**

Left **The coast near Kīhei** Right **Four Seasons Resort Lāna'i, The Lodge at Kō'ele**

Key to abbreviations
Adm *admission charge payable* **Free** *no admission charge*

MAUI'S
TOP 10

MAUI'S TOP 10

TOP 10 Maui's Highlights

Maui is known as the "valley isle", and most of its population nestles in the low-lying isthmus between the lush western mountains and the dustier slopes of Haleakalā to the east. Skirting the coast are some of the world's finest beaches, from the popular resorts on the south-western fringe to the wilder surfing beaches on the north and eastern shores. Maui's administrative group also includes the islands of Moloka'i and Lana'i with more magnificent scenery and even greater remoteness.

1 Front Street Lahaina

The well-preserved buildings along this street take you back to the early 1800s, when missionaries arrived to save the souls of bawdy sailors and bring Christianity to islanders. *(See pp8–9.)*

2 'Iao Valley & Kepaniwai Park Gardens

Up in the verdant 'Iao Valley, the Kepaniwai Park Gardens celebrate the diverse cultures that make up modern Maui through a range of national gardens and structures. *(See pp10–11.)*

3 Wailuku and Kahului

These twin towns are where the majority of Maui's populace live and work. The area also has fantastic sights, from missionary churches to ancient sites to lush, tropical plantations. *(See pp12–13.)*

4 Bailey House Museum

A fascinating place, focusing on 19th-century missionary life, and the earlier Hawaiian culture, which missionaries attempted to dispel. *(See pp14–15.)*

5 Mākena

Once the remotest spot on Maui's southern coast, Mākena has become increasingly popular with divers in recent years. *(See pp16–17.)*

Map labels: Honokōhau Bay, Honokōhau, Kapalua, Napili, Kahana, Honokōwai, Ka'anapali, Kahakuloa, Waihe'e, Kahului Bay, Spreckelsville, West Maui Mountains, KAHEKILI HWY, 'Iao Valley & Kepaniwai Park, Lahaina, Wailuku & Kahului, Pu'unēnē, HALEAKALĀ, HONOAPI'ILANI HWY, Waikapū, Waikapū, MOKULELE HWY, Keahuaiwi, Olowalu, Pāpalaua, Punahoa Beach, 'Au'au Channel, Mā'alaea, Mā'alaea Bay, Kīhei, Waipuilani, Kama'ole, Wailea, Polo Beach Park, Mākena, 'Āhihi Bay, 'Ulupalakua Ranch, La Pérouse Bay

Share your travel recommendations on traveldk.com

'Ulupalakua Ranch

6 On the southern slopes of Haleakalā, this ranch is the locale of the Tedeschi Vineyards. Before the introduction of vines, the winery experimented with a pineapple wine, Maui Blanc. *(See pp18–19.)*

Haleakalā National Park

7 The amazingly diverse terrain of this national park – from rain forest to desert – culminates in the moon-like landscape of Haleakalā's enormous crater. *(See pp20–21.)*

The Road to Hāna

8 Fifty-six miles of winding coastal road, with jaw-dropping ocean views to the left and sparkling waterfalls amid shady woodlands to the right. *(See pp22–3.)*

Kīpahulu and Kaupō

9 On the wild and beautiful east coast of Maui, this area offers fantastic treks through forest paths to discover spectacular falls and revitalising mountain pools. *(See pp24–5.)*

Kalaupapa National Park, Moloka'i

10 On the "get-away-from-it-all" island of Moloka'i, Kalaupapa is an isolated peninsula, flat as a golf green and separated from the rest of the island by sheer cliffs. Formerly, it was used as a leper colony. *(See pp26–7.)*

Front Street, Lahaina

Listed on the National Register of Historic Places, the main thoroughfare of Lahaina is a showcase of restored and preserved sites. In the early 1800s, when this seaside village was the capital of the Hawaiian Kingdom, missionaries from New England arrived, determined to save the souls of native islanders and to discipline rowdy sailors. There's no proof that souls were saved but the buildings of the era have been.

Statue at the
Pioneer Inn

Banyan Tree

🌀 Front Street is a great place for treasure hunters to find scrimshaw, t-shirts, sarongs, and souvenirs. You can meet local artists and crafters who sell their works under the Banyan Tree on weekends.

🌀 Parking is at a premium along Front Street, and it's easier to park in a pay lot.

🌀 "Lahaina" means merciless sun in the Hawaiian language, a good indication that you should wear your hat and sunscreen when strolling along Front Street.

- Map C3
- Visitor Center, Lahaina Courthouse; 9am–5pm daily; free
- Baldwin House; 10am–4pm daily; adm $3
- Wo Hing Temple; 10am–4pm daily; donation
- Jodo Mission; grounds open daily; free

Top 10 Sights

1. Lahaina Courthouse
2. Banyan Tree
3. Lahaina Harbor
4. Hau'ola Stone
5. Pioneer Inn
6. Baldwin House
7. Wo Hing Temple
8. U.S. Seamen's Hospital
9. Jodo Mission
10. Moku'ula

Lahaina Courthouse
Built from coral blocks in 1859, the courthouse *(above)* also housed the local prison. The former jail cells are now used to display the work of local artists, and there's a visitor center here, too.

Banyan Tree
Planted in 1873 by the Sheriff of Maui to mark the 50th anniversary of the founding of Lahaina's first Christian mission, the Banyan Tree is the center of the town's activity – festivals, concerts, arts and crafts fairs, and daily socializing take place under the shade of this venerated tree.

Pionner Inn

Lahaina Harbor
Where whaling ships once laid anchor, charter fishing vessels now troll for a catch of delicious *ahi*, *ono*, and *mahimahi*. Other boats wait to take visitors on snorkeling expeditions, whale-watching excursions, and trips to Lāna'i and Moloka'i.

4 Hau'ola Stone
Hawaiians have a deep relationship with their natural surroundings, including stones, or *pōhaku*. Those deemed as healing stones, like the one near Lahaina Library, were believed to hold powerful forces of nature that could quiet the spirit and heal the soul.

5 Pioneer Inn
You can still rent a room in this landmark, which for many years was the only hotel in town. It was built in 1901 by a Royal Canadian Mountie who tracked a notorious criminal to Lahaina and then decided to stay. It has a perfect view of the Harbor. *(See p120.)*

6 Baldwin House
Constructed in 1834 for New England missionary Rev. Dwight Baldwin, the faithfully restored house is now a museum that presents a vivid picture of missionary life in the 1800s.

7 Wo Hing Temple
Chinese sugar plantation laborers built this fraternal hall *(above)* in the 19th century. It now holds a collection of everyday utensils used by the immigrant workers, and shows movies of Hawai'i taken in the early 20th century by Thomas Edison. *(See p57.)*

9 Jodo Mission
The Jodo Mission *(above)* commemorates the arrival of the first Japanese immigrants to Maui in 1868. The largest statue of Buddha outside of Japan sits majestically and serenely in the grounds. *(See p59.)*

8 U.S. Seamen's Hospital
Originally built for Kamehameha III *(see p31)*, the US government leased the building for use as a marine hospital. The whaling industry created a need throughout the Pacific for hospitals to care for injured, sick, and abandoned sailors.

10 Moku'ula
There used to be a lake on this site, and in it an island, Moku'ula, which was home to Hawaiian royalty. In 1918, the lake was filled in, and the island is now buried under the sports facilities of Malu-'ulu'olele County Park.

The Mo'o (Lizard) of Moku'ula
As well as providing a base for the Hawaiian royalty of the 19th century, Moku'ula and its surrounding waters were home to a legendary lizard that was worshiped by the royal family as a special guardian of this sacred spot.

For more on Lahaina see pp56–61

9

TOP 10 'Īao Valley and Kepaniwai Park Gardens

Tales of long ago warfare linger in the mists that crown the velvety green crags rising above 'Īao Valley. In this now-tranquil spot, Maui warriors fell while defending the island from the invading Kamehameha I. Kepaniwai – literally, "the water dam" – refers to the damming of 'Īao Stream by the bodies of the vanquished. In ancient times, access to the valley was restricted to ali'i (royalty); today, it is a state park and one of Maui's most visited sites.

Statue of Japanese farm laborers

Hiking path

🌀 When hiking, wear a swimsuit under your shorts so that you can take a refreshing dip in 'Īao Stream.

🚫 There are no restaurants in the immediate vicinity, so stop in Wailuku and pick up a plate lunch to enjoy at the picnic tables in Kepaniwai Park

• Map D3
• Maui Visitors Bureau, 244 3530; www.visitmaui.com
• Kepaniwai Park; 7am–7pm daily; free
• Hawai'i Nature Center, 'Īao Valley Rd.; 244 6500; 10am–4pm daily; guided hikes available
• Adm $6

Top 10 Sights

1. 'Īao Needle
2. 'Īao Stream
3. Hiking Paths
4. Precontact Hawaiian Settlement
5. Japanese Tea House and Garden
6. Chinese Pagoda
7. Missionary New England Salt Box
8. Portugese Villa
9. Picnic Area
10. Hawai'i Nature Center

1 'Īao Needle

Legend has it that 'Īao was the beautiful daughter of demigod Māui and his wife Hina. Though strictly forbidden, a young warrior became 'Īao's lover. Māui found out, and punished the man by turning him into a pillar of stone, now known as the 'Īao Needle.

Japanese Garden

2 'Īao Stream

The largest of the major streams reaching the ocean from Pu'u Kukui (West Maui Mountains), 'Īao forms one of Nā Wai 'Ehā (The Four Waters) valleys of Maui. There are several pools along the stream that are easily accessible for a refreshing dip in the cool water.

3 Hiking Paths

Crisscrossing the valley, most of the park's hiking paths are well maintained. A leisurely walk to the top takes about half an hour, and markers along the way note historic battles.

Sign up for DK's email newsletter on traveldk.com

4 Precontact Hawaiian Settlement

Along the river, under ferns, camouflaged by moss and overgrown by invasive coffee plants, one can find remnants of the stone foundations of early Hawaiian village sites *(right)*. Also visible are farming terraces typical of traditional Hawaiian agriculture.

5 Japanese Tea House and Garden

The beautiful Japanese Garden, centered around a traditional tea house, reflects a culture that also shows itself in Hawaiian customs, such as removing shoes before entering a home.

6 Chinese Pagoda

The Chinese Pagoda celebrates the culture of the laborers who were brought to work on Maui's sugar plantations in the 1850s. The Chinese influence continues today in culinary treats, such as *manapua* (steamed buns).

7 Missionary New England Salt Box

The architecture of the colonial United States, with its predominance of white-painted wooden structures (the "salt box" form), was brought by Protestant missionaries, who came to the Hawaiian islands beginning in the 1820s.

9 Picnic Area

Pick up a plate lunch and a soft drink at any of the myriad local restaurants and snack bars in Wailuku, and enjoy it at the picnic tables located in a shady grove near ʻĪao Stream. The tables are sheltered from the sun and are easily accessible from the parking lot.

8 Portuguese Villa

The Portuguese came in the late 19th century and taught the Hawaiians how to tend cattle and other livestock. Outside the villa is a traditional stone bread oven *(left)*. Portuguese bread is very popular in Maui today.

10 Hawaiʻi Nature Center

At this well-planned educational attraction, you can wiggle your fingers in a touch pool, play evolutionary roulette, and try to guess how many plants and animals chanced upon the Hawaiian islands.

Kepaniwai's Story

Kepaniwai Park was established in 1952 to showcase and celebrate Maui's cultural diversity. Traditional houses and gardens of each ethnic group that settled on the island are located throughout the park. Its latest addition is the Korean pavilion, constructed in 2003 to commemorate 100 years of Korean immigration to Hawaiʻi.

TOP10 Wailuku and Kahului

Wailuku, Maui's County seat, and Kahului, the island's business and retail center, are nestled between Pu'u Kukui (West Maui Mountains) and Haleakalā. For centuries this area has been the center of power and population on Maui, and today it offers a vast array of culture, history, nature, entertainment, dining, shopping, and recreation. As the gateway to Maui, Kahului is also home to the island's largest airport and primary harbor.

Kanahā Beach

Central Maui is the place to go for a short day of sightseeing. All the attractions are within short distances of each other.

Find a large assortment of books about Maui and local handicrafts at the Bailey House Museum shop.

Some of the best cheap eats on the island are located in Wailuku – at the top of the list are Sam Sato's, Wei Wei BBQ, Maui Bake Shop, Tokyo Tei, A.K.'s Café, Saeng Thai, and Asian Star.

• Map E3 • Maui Tropical Plantation, Waikapu; 244 7643; 9am–5pm daily; free; adm for tram $14, under 12 $5
• Alexander & Baldwin Sugar Museum, Pū'ūnene; 871 8058; 9:30am–4:30pm Mon–Sat; adm $7, children 6–12 $2
• Maui Arts & Cultural Center, Kahului; 242 7469

Top 10 Sights

1. Market Street
2. Ka'ahumanu Church
3. Wailuku Public Library
4. Maui Tropical Plantation
5. Alexander & Baldwin Sugar Museum
6. Kanahā Pond
7. Keōpū'olani Park
8. Maui Arts & Cultural Center
9. War Memorial Park
10. Haleki'i and Pihana Heiau

2 Ka'ahumanu Church

This smart, white, steeple-topped church mirrored the establishment of Christianity in Hawai'i. It began as a grass hut, progressed to an adobe structure, was replaced by stone in 1837, and rebuilt in its present form in 1876. It was spruced up again in the 1970s. (See p71.)

3 Wailuku Public Library

Wailuku Library (1928, above) and the neighboring Territorial Building (1931) were designed by C.W. Dickey, the architect credited with developing the Hawaiian style, characterized by a double-hipped roof.

1 Market Street

Nowhere is the small-town charm of Wailuku more evident than on Market Street. Here you can find unusual boutiques, antique shops, local art galleries, and the 1920s' pink 'Īao Theater, which hosts community stage productions.

Ka'ahumanu Church

4 Maui Tropical Plantation

Here, a tram takes you on an exotic journey of the senses through fields of sugar cane, and plantations of pineapples, bananas, mangoes, papaya, and macadamia nuts. This working farm (below) also has a gift shop and a restaurant on site. (See p71.)

5 Alexander & Baldwin Sugar Museum

This award-winning museum, housed in a period residence, presents a lively look at Maui's plantation life through interactive displays, photos, and artifacts. (See p72.)

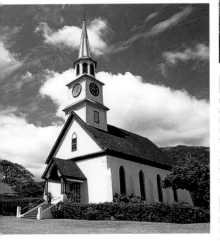

6 Kanahā Pond

As well as providing respite for migrating ducks and geese, Kanahā Pond is also home to the Hawaiian stilt (ae'o) and the Hawaiian coot (alae ke'oke'o), both endangered species. They can be seen from an observation shelter just off Route 37.

7 Keōpū'olani Park

Fronting the ocean, this beautiful 101-acre park has many paths that meander through broad green lawns, a native botanical garden, a croquet course (for public use), a skate park, and a playground.

8 Maui Arts & Cultural Center

The MACC (left) presents an almost daily schedule of performances and exhibitions, and its 1,200-seat Castle Theater regularly shows independent and classic films. (See p74.)

9 War Memorial Park

Honoring the servicemen and women of Maui County who have given their lives for their country, this complex is the site of many athletic and community events. Each fall, the grounds are transformed into a maze of booths, tents, and livestock for the Maui County Fair. (See p37.)

10 Haleki'i and Pihana Heiau

Two of Maui's most impressive archeological sites. Haleki'i (literally, "image house") was a chiefly compound; Pihana, a luakini (temple), where human sacrifices were offered. There are also magnificent views here of Haleakalā and 'Īao Valley.

A Human Dam

In 1790, the mighty Kamehameha the Great defeated Maui's ruling chief, Kahekili, in a bloody battle at Kepaniwai in 'Īao Valley. Kepaniwai ("the damming of the waters") refers to the blocking of 'Īao Stream by bodies of defeated Maui warriors. Grateful for victory, Kamehameha is said to have offered a human sacrifice at nearby Pihana Heiau.

⑩ Bailey House Museum

This former girls' school was established in 1832 on the site of the royal compound of Kahekili, the last ruling chief of Maui. Christian missionary teachers Edward and Caroline Bailey came here to teach their language, customs, and religion to young Hawaiian women. The building is now a museum with exhibits showcasing both traditional Hawaiian and missionary life.

Exotic foliage, Bailey House Gardens

Gardens

🕒 The Museum shop is an excellent place to buy gifts. It has a wide selection of books about Hawai'i and work by local artisans.

🍴 There is no restaurant on the grounds, but visitors are welcome to bring food to enjoy outside on the shady lawn.

• Map N2
• 2375A Main Street, Wailuku
• www.mauimuseum.org
• 244 3326
• 10am–4pm Mon–Sat
• Closed Sun and major holidays
• Adm $5; children 7–12 $1; under 6 free

Top 10 Highlights

1. Bailey's Original Oil Paintings
2. Bailey's Sugar Mill
3. Bailey's Aqueduct
4. Precontact Artifacts
5. Missionary Artifacts
6. Historic Archives
7. Outrigger Canoe
8. Kapa Display
9. Hawaiian Land Snails Collection
10. Gardens

1 Bailey's Original Oil Paintings

Bailey's paintings may not have sold well enough to help him financially, but they have provided an accurate and fascinating record of Maui in the 19th century. He did not have formal training, but visiting artists encouraged him to take up oils. The landscapes of Wailuku were exhibited in San Francisco, Philadelphia, and Paris in the 1870s.

2 Bailey's Sugar Mill

In the 1860s, Bailey attempted to support his family by growing and milling sugar cane on this site, an endeavor that proved too small to be profitable. The Bailey and Sons Plantation later became part of Wailuku Sugar Company.

3 Bailey's Aqueduct

The stone waterworks still visible adjoining the house were built by Bailey to bring water from 'Iao Stream to run his sugar mill.

Bailey House

4 Precontact Artifacts

The museum houses an outstanding collection of more than 1,000 ancient Hawaiian artifacts *(left)* dating from the time before Western contact was made. There are pieces made of bone, stone and feathers, as well as practical items such as bowls and fish hooks.

5 Missionary Artifacts

The exhibits offer a glimpse of missionary life through furniture, clothing, quilts, and cooking utensils. The koa table was to be a gift for U.S. President Ulysses S. Grant in 1869, but Congress forbade the president from accepting gifts from foreign nations.

6 Historic Archives

A fascinating trawl of photographs, books, newspapers, and maps of Maui dating back to the 1880s. Documents include a letter from Samuel Clemens – aka 19th-century author Mark Twain – and detailed charts of the island's archaeological sites.

7 Outrigger Canoe

Hōnaunau (above) is a 200-year-old fishing canoe built from a single koa log. During Hawai'i's "Beach Boy Era" of the 1930s and '40s, the canoe was used by the Outrigger Canoe Club in Waikīkī. It is proudly displayed in a separate *hale*, or house, outside the main building.

8 Kapa Display

Kapa is a traditional cloth made from the bark of the paper mulberry tree, and its production was the preserve of women in old Hawai'i. The clothing, blankets, and capes on display are imprinted with the signatures of the women, who created their own designs with plant dyes.

10 Gardens

Many of the plants in the gardens (below) had medicinal uses in old Hawai'i. 'Uki'uki, used to dye kapa, grew in 'Īao Valley before settlers changed Hawai'i's natural vegetation.

9 Hawaiian Land Snails Collection

Dwight David Baldwin began his collection of 1,144 specimens, most found only in Hawaii, in 1873. Many of the snails on display represent species that are now extinct.

Bailey's Projects

Bailey bought his homestead and adjoining land in 1850, following the school's closure the year before. When the mission cut off his funding, Bailey struggled on by selling landscape paintings, surveying land for the Kingdom of Hawai'i, supervising road and bridge construction, growing and milling sugar cane, and supervising government schools.

TOP10 Mākena

Hawaiian villages once lined most of the southern coast of Maui, but the lava flow from Haleakalā coupled with the arrival of Westerners reduced the area's population. For many years, this was the island's "end of the road" and its biggest attraction was Big Beach, the long expanse of white sand at Oneloa. However, the area has seen residential development recently and has become increasingly popular with divers and kayakers.

La Pérouse Memorial

Coastel view

🌀 Don't leave valuables in your car. If you plan to hike, wear sturdy shoes – *'a'ā* lava is very sharp – and take plenty of water as Mākena is always hot and dry.

Fill up the car in Kīhei and pack a picnic because once you pass the Maui Prince Hotel, there are no services.

• Map E5
• Maui Visitors Bureau 244 3530
• *'Āhihi-Kina'u Natural Reserve*; free access
• Snorkeling excursions to Molokini depart from both Mā'alaea and Lahaina harbors: try Maui Classic Charters (879 8188) from Mā'alaea, or Lahaina Princess (667 6165) from Lahaina

Top 10 Sights

1. La Pérouse Memorial
2. 'Āhihi-Kina'u Natural Reserve
3. Remains of Pre-Contact Hawaiian Coastal Villages
4. Kīpuka
5. Mt. Haleakalā's Last Lava Flow
6. Rare Hawaiian Dry Land Plants
7. Hoapili Trail (King's Trail)
8. Pu'uōla'i
9. Molokini
10. Kaho'olawe

1 La Pérouse Memorial

French Admiral Jean-Francois Galaup Comte de la Pérouse was the first European navigator known to land on Maui. Commanding two frigates, La Boussole and Lastrolabe, he sailed into the bay that now bears his name on May 30, 1786. This area, known as Keone'ō'io, was well populated at the time, but La Pérouse's monument now stands alone in a lava field at the edge of the bay.

Mākena Beach

2 'Āhihi-Kina'u Natural Reserve

Hawai'i's only natural preserve to include a marine component, this coastal area is a mix of marine life habitats, archaeological sites, and geological features, such as lava tide pools, coastal lava tubes, and fields of *'a'ā* (rough lava).

3 Remains of Pre-contact Hawaiian Coastal Villages

Two hundred years ago, this was a bustling region, with four fishing villages and a *heiau* (religious temple). The remains of these coastal settlements (consisting mostly of walled and terraced platforms) are visible among the lava flows *(above right)*.

4 Kīpuka

Throughout 'Āhihi-Kina'u preserve, there are islands of untouched ground *(kīpuka)* within the lava fields, caused when lava flows around raised areas of the landscape.

5 Mt. Haleakalā's Last Lava Flow

Haleakalā last erupted in 1790. La Pérouse's first landing preceded the eruption, and when he returned in 1790 he found that the large settlement of Keone'ō'io had been destroyed, and the bay bisected by the large finger of lava that can be seen today.

6 Rare Hawaiian Dry Land Plants

Volcanic rock may not seem like a good medium for plant growth, but hardened lava and loose cinders are rich in nutrients, and many native species thrive in this environment.

7 Hoapili Trail (King's Trail)

This trail follows the remnants of the stone-paved Hoapili (King's) Highway, which once encircled the entire island of Maui. Ancient house platforms, *heiau*, and other archaeological sites are visible along the trail that winds from the sea, up the mountain, and back down along the coastline.

9 Molokini

This crescent-shaped, submerged volcanic crater *(above)* off the south shore is one of Hawaii's most popular snorkeling and scuba spots *(see pp44–5)*. Numerous charter boats visit daily, bringing visitors to experience the clear waters and abundant sea life. The steep crater walls are thronged with chattering sea birds.

8 Pu'uōla'i

This cone-shaped hill, formed in Haleakalā's last lava flow, separates Mākena's most popular beaches, Oneloa and "Little Beach." Folklore has it that Pu'uōla'i is the tail of a *mo'o*, or lizard, who angered the fire goddess Pele.

10 Kaho'olawe

Rising from the sea off the Mākena coast is Kaho'olawe. Uninhabited since its days as a practice missile target, it was once a thriving community, as the dozens of *heiau* (temples) attest. (See also p31.)

Kaho'olawe Today

Kaho'olawe now serves as a cultural retreat for the pursuit and education of traditional Hawaiian customs, beliefs, and practices. Currently access is restricted to one visit a month, arranged by the Protect Kaho'olawe 'Ohana (www.kahoolawe.org). Generally, however, the trips are not open to visitors.

ᴛᴏᴘ10 'Ulupalakua Ranch

Stretching across Haleakalā's southern flank, the 'Ulupalakua Ranch contains a winery and also a memorial park to the Honolulu-educated Chinese revolutionary Dr. Sun Yat-sen. Whaling Captain James Makee acquired the land in 1856 and built a cottage for King Kalākaua, the "Merrie Monarch." The current owner bought the property in 1963 and has used it for farming cattle.

Wine tasting

Ranch sign

🕐 The Tedeschi Winery happily packages their wine for easy shipment home.

🍔 Try a hamburger of fresh-ground ranch beef at the 'Ulupalakua Store.

• Map F5
• 878 6058
• info@mauiwine.com
• www.mauiwine.com
• Tasting room 10am–5pm daily
• Free tours of winery daily at 10:30am, 1:30pm, and 3pm

Top 10 Sights

1. Dr. Sun Yat-sen Memorial Park
2. Tedeschi Vineyards
3. Tedeschi Winery
4. King Kalākaua's Cottage
5. History Room
6. Coral Prison
7. Makee Sugar Mill
8. Giant Camphor Tree
9. Capt. Makee's Cannon
10. Ranch Store & Cowboys

1 Dr. Sun Yat-sen Memorial Park

The ranch donated the land for a small memorial park in Keokea, en route to the winery. It contains a bronze statue of Sun Yat-sen and was dedicated on the late doctor's birthday in 1989. When he was wanted "dead or alive" in China for his revolutionary activities, Sun Yat-sen sought refuge with his brother, who had a farm near the site. The memorial also commemorates the bicentennial of the first Chinese immigrants to Hawai'i. *(See p87.)*

The giant camphor tree

2 Tedeschi Vineyards

Some 20 acres of hybrid carnelian grapes grow on the sunny leeward slope of Haleakalā – the fruit destined for the vats of Maui's only commercial winery.

3 Tedeschi Winery

The winery *(tasting room left)* made its first product, Maui Blanc, from Hawai'i's best-known fruit – pineapples! Grapes were harvested in 1980 and turned into sparkling wine, Maui Brut-Blanc de Noirs, which was served at the inauguration of President Ronald Reagan. Maui Blush, Maui Nouveau, Rose Ranch Cuvee, Maui Splash, 'Ulupalakua Red, and Plantation Red have since been added to the list.

Sign up for DK's email newsletter on traveldk.com

4 King Kalākaua's Cottage

King Kalākaua's taste for champagne was legendary, and so it is fitting that the cottage built for him in 1874 is now the winery's Tasting Room. The centerpiece is an 18-ft bar cut from the trunk of a mango tree *(left)* where visitors can sample products.

5 History Room

Also in the King's Cottage is the History Room *(right)*, which contains photos and artifacts of the ranch's most renowned owners, the story of Maui's *paniolo* (cowboys), and tales of polo ponies.

6 Coral Prison

One of the ranch's original buildings has stout walls made of coral and may once have been used as a jail for rowdy ranch hands who were lowered through a trap door to the "keep" below.

7 Makee Sugar Mill

Ruins of the mill's stone chimney are still visible across the street from the Tasting Room.

8 Giant Camphor Tree

This huge tree, more than 150 years old, was part of Makee's original landscaping. Many plants, trees, and shrubs were imported by Makee to make his home the "showcase of Maui." It's believed the Makee family introduced more types of ornamental trees and shrubs to Hawai'i than any other person or organization.

9 Capt. Makee's Cannon

When King Kalākaua's ship was sighted entering Mākena Bay, Makee would fire his cannon *(below)* to let the ship's crew know that a greeting party would soon be there to welcome the visiting monarch. Alas, the cannon no longer issues welcoming salvos.

10 Ranch Store and Cowboys

Whimsical, life-sized sculptures of lanky cowboys *(above)* by the late local artist Reems Mitchell welcome visitors from the porch of the small country store. Snacks, sundries, and souvenirs with a *paniolo* (cowboy) theme are available.

The Rose and the Breadfruit

Captain James Makee named the property Rose Ranch after his wife Catherine's favorite flower. Current owner C. Pardee Erdman named it 'Ulupalakua Ranch after the district name. 'Ulupalakua means "breadfruit ripened on the back," a reference to the days when chiefs' messengers carried the fruit from Hāna.

🔟 Haleakalā National Park

This stunning park encompasses rain forests, desert, and subtropical beaches, but the lunar-like landscape of Haleakalā's crater is the main attraction. This is the world's most voluminous dormant volcano, its crater large enough to hold the entire island of Manhattan. The park's entrance is at the 7,000-ft level, and lies at the end of a road that winds up from sea level in 37 miles of scenic switchbacks. There are hiking trails, campgrounds, and three cabins in the park.

Hosmer Grove

🍃 Be prepared. It can be extremely cold at the summit (especially at sunrise), the air is thin, and the sun very strong. Conditions can change very rapidly, so take warm clothes, rain gear, sunscreen, and something hot to drink.

🚫 There are no restaurants within the park, so stop en route to the park or pack a picnic lunch; of course, carry plenty of drinking water.

• Map J5
• Park HQ Visitor Center 572 4400; 6:30am–4pm; $10 per car, $5 per bike; camping is limited, cabins available by reservation only – go to https://fhnp.org/wcr
• Haleakalā Visitor Center is inside the park at the 9,700-ft level
• www.nps.gov/hale

Top 10 Sights
1 Visitor Centers
2 Hosmer Grove
3 Leleiwi Overlook
4 Nēnē
5 Pu'u 'Ula'ula Summit
6 Sliding Sands Trail
7 Halemau'u Trail
8 Pele's Paint Pot
9 Silversword Loop
10 Kaupō Trail

Visitor Centers
The Park HQ (for camping permits and info) is one mile from the park entrance. The Haleakalā Visitor Center is 10 miles farther up and has a good supply of maps and books, but no phone, gas, or food.

Hosmer Grove
Take the first left turn just beyond the park entrance to Hosmer Grove. Home to many native and alien bird, plant, and insect species, it's one of Maui's best nature-watching spots. A short trail winds through the stands of cedar, pine, and other trees introduced in the 19th century.

Leleiwi Overlook
Located six miles above Park HQ, the overlook offers an amazing view of the crater *(below)*. From here, on rare occasions in late afternoon, your own shadow can be seen on clouds in the crater, the image surrounded by a rainbow.

Pu'u 'Ula'ula Summit

Nēnē
Hawai'i's state bird *(above)*, making a comeback from the brink of extinction, can be seen on the slopes of Haleakalā and sometimes in the visitor center parking lot. The birds resemble the Canada Goose but are usually smaller; males and females have identical plumage.

5 Pu'u 'Ula'ula Summit

Nowhere is the view more spectacular than from this highest point on Maui. Minimal relief from the cold wind can be found in the glassed-in observation house. There, you can also find out about the expansive view, which includes the volcanic peaks on Hawai'i. On clear days, Kaua'i is the only main Hawaiian island not visible.

6 Sliding Sands Trail

From the Visitor Center, this 5-mile trail (left) descends through several climatic zones, including a barren cinder desert and alpine shrub land. The return ascent is steep and hard going.

7 Halemau'u Trail

With many switchbacks, this 10-mile trail (above) is not for the faint of heart but does offer magnificent views down to the ocean. It begins at the 8,000-ft level and descends quickly to the crater floor, passing Hōlua Cabin, Silversword Loop, and the Bottomless Pit.

8 Pele's Paint Pot

Along the Halemau'u Trail, this surreal landscape of brilliantly colored ash owes its magnificent hues to volcanic mineral deposits and equally colorful cinder cones rising from the crater floor.

9 Silversword Loop

One of the world's rarest plants, Haleakalā Silversword ('ahinahina) appears on this trail (below). It's a very rare sight, though, blooming only once, with a spectacular 6-ft stalk of purple flowers; it then dies.

10 Kaupō Trail

This challenging 18-mile trek traverses the crater floor, then progresses through the rain forest in the southern valley. Hikers should arrange for a ride back from the trail's end, at the beautiful but very remote Kaupō.

The Topography

The park encompasses dry forests, rain forests, desert, and subtropical beaches centered around the mighty crater, 3,000 ft deep and with a circumference of some 21 miles. Two competing forces of nature created the crater: volcanism (which formed the mountain) and erosion (which sculpted the depression).

For more on these treks, as well as others throughout Maui see pp40–41

The Road to Hāna

A highway in name only, the famous road from Kahului to Hāna winds along the coastline for 56 miles, offering panoramic ocean views and passing by waterfalls, pools, lush gardens, and parks. The mostly two-lane road traverses 54 bridges and 617 curves (yes, someone really did count them!). Hāna itself has retained a pristine beauty and many old Hawaiian ways.

Hāna Highway

Fruit stall on Hāna Highway

🕗 Don't be in a hurry – allow a full day for the round trip. Pull over and let others pass as you enjoy the scenery, or take a dip in one of the refreshing pools formed by the waterfalls that cascade alongside the road.

🍴 Pack a picnic and stop at any one of the many roadside parks. Once you've left Pāʻia, there are no services along Hāna Highway and not very many once you reach Hāna.

• Kahanu Gardens (Map K4) Mon–Fri 10am–2pm, 248 8912
• Adm $10
• Hāna Cultural Center (Map L4), 10am–4pm Mon–Sat, 248 8622
• Adm $3
• Hasegawa General Store, Hāna (Map L4), 248 8231
• Maui Visitors Bureau 244 3530

Top 10 Sights

1. Honomanū Bay
2. Keʻanae Peninsula
3. Coral Miracle Church, Wailua
4. Kahanu Gardens
5. Piʻilanihale Heiau
6. Kaʻeleku Cave
7. Paʻiloa Beach
8. Kauʻiki Hill
9. Hāna Cultural Center
10. Hasegawa General Store

Wailua from the highway

Honomanū Bay

There are no facilities here but it is a popular site with surfers and fishermen. Though the offshore currents are too strong for swimming, the scenery is absolutely terrific, with steep cliffs backing the bay, covered with an abundance of tropical foliage *(above)*.

Keʻanae Peninsula

The lush patchwork of taro fields *(see p50)* is the enduring characteristic of the peninsula. Standing out against the greenery is Keʻanae Congregational Church. Built of lava rock and coral mortar, it was the only building left standing after a tsunami (tidal wave) hit in 1946.

Coral Miracle Church, Wailua

The church *(below)* gets its name from a "miraculous" storm that, in 1860, pitched up the coral of the building's construction on a nearby beach. Previously the rock had to be retrieved by hand from the ocean's depths. A further miracle helpfully lapped up the leftover coral, clearing the beach again.

For advice about driving in Hawaiʻi, see p108

Honomanū Bay

1 **2** Ke'anae Peninsula

3 Wailua
Wailua Bay
Nāhiku
HĀNA HIGHWAY

4 **5**
7 Pailoa Beach
6
Kau'iki Hill **8**
9 **10**
Hāna

4 Kahanu Gardens
A branch of the National Tropical Botanical Garden, the 472 acres of Kahanu Gardens encompass breadfruit trees, coconut palms, and a host of other Pacific Island plants. The gardens are not merely beautiful, for they focus on plants most culturally valued by Polynesians.

5 Pi'ilanihale Heiau
The largest and best-preserved heiau (religious site) in the state of Hawai'i, the 50-ft monument was built for (and possibly by) a 16th-century chief.

6 Ka'eleku Cave
This is the only cave on Maui open to the public, though, like all other "caves" in Hawai'i, it is actually a lava tube. Dark and cool, there are stalactites and stalagmites as you might encounter in other caves, only here they are formed of lava.

7 Pa'iloa Beach
Located within Wai'ānapanapa State Park, this pitch-black sand beach (below) was formed by ancient volcanic action and is quite spectacular. Pa'iloa is surrounded by lava pinnacles, and the area is great for walks.

8 Kau'iki Hill
Steeped in history and crowned with mist, this volcanic point was a valued defensive site in Hawai'i's warring past. Said to be the home of the demigod Māui, a small, red sand beach and a lighthouse now mark this prominent point on Hāna Bay.

9 Hāna Cultural Center
The cultural center (above) houses, through artifacts, books, and photographs, the history of Hāna's people. The culture is palpably infused within the quilts, cooking utensils, instruments, fish hooks, coconut graters, stone lamps, and gourd bowls.

10 Hasegawa General Store
A famous landmark in this part of the world, the store was established almost 100 years ago. Selling life's necessities, from groceries to fishing gear, its organic dried fruit, coffee, and macadamia nuts are all grown close by.

Hāna's Past
In precontact times, Hāna was a large settlement and the birthplace of Queen Ka'ahumanu. Before the Hāna Highway was completed in 1927 only a horse trail connected this end of the island to the rest. Sugar cane plantations were converted to a cattle ranch in 1946. Shortly after that, the area's only hotel, the Hāna-Maui, was built.

For details about the Hotel Hāna-Maui, see p116

⑩ Kīpahulu and Kaupō

Long before the first Europeans arrived on Maui, the Kīpahulu district was prized by the Hawaiian ali'i (royalty) for its fertile land and bountiful sea. Thousands of people lived in the villages of Hāna, Kīpahulu, and Kaupō, sustaining themselves through farming and fishing. Beyond Hāna, the road continues through Kīpahulu, Kaupō, and finally, winds its way up to 'Ulupalakua, offering spectacular scenery and the serenity that comes with an almost non-existent human population.

Waimoku Falls

Kaupō coast

🗸 If you plan to drive around Maui's "backside," make sure you have food, water, and plenty of gas when you leave Hāna. The next populated area is 'Ulupalakua in Upcountry Maui.

As tempting as it may be, do not take any stones or other natural objects from Haleakalā National Park as souvenirs.

• Map K5–J6
• Kīpahulu Ranger Station & Visitor Center: 248 7375
• Maui Visitors Bureau: 244 3530

Top 10 Sights

1. 'Ohe'o Gulch
2. Seven Pools
3. Falls at Makahiku
4. Waimoku Falls
5. Charles Lindbergh's Grave
6. Kīpahulu Point Lighthouse County Park
7. Hui Aloha Church, Kaupō
8. Kaupō Store
9. St. Joseph's Church
10. Kaupō Gap

'Ohe'o Gulch

The Kīpahulu Valley, formed by the flowing waters of 'Ohe'o Gulch, drops steeply from the east rim of Haleakalā to the ocean. A rain forest wilderness, its fragile environment is mostly protected as a preserve and closed to the public. But the lower part of the valley can be visited on foot along the Waimoku Falls Trail.

Seven Pools

Many more than seven pools, in fact, all formed by the waterfalls rushing seaward from the top of Haleakalā. This lush tropical area *(right)* is great for hiking, swimming, and camping. The pools below the road are easy to reach, but more adventurous visitors search out the upper pools along the Waimoku Falls Trail.

One of the Seven Pools

Falls at Makahiku

These magnificent 181-ft falls are accessible from the Waimoku Falls Trail (half a mile up from 'Ohe'o Gulch ranger station). A beautiful pool at the top of the falls is great for a cooling dip.

Waimoku Falls

Farther up the trail, beyond a fantastic bamboo forest, Waimoku Falls spills 450 ft over the ledge of a high cliff, tumbling into a shallow pool. You can swim or wade in the refreshing water here, a welcome treat on a hot day.

Charles Lindbergh's Grave

First to fly solo across the Atlantic, Charles Lindbergh (1902–74), lived out his days amid the peaceful beauty of the Hāna coast. He sketched the design for his grave, which lies behind the Palapala Ho'omau Church in Kīpahulu.

Kīpahulu Point Lighthouse County Park

Right by the site of Lindbergh's grave is this pleasant little park. Formerly the surrounds of a working lighthouse, the park's shady trees and tables overlook the ocean, making it ideal for picnics.

Huialoha Church, Kaupō

Built in 1859, the church fell into disrepair during the last century. However, volunteers worked to renovate the building and it was reopened in 1978, adding extra meaning to its name Huialoha, "meeting of compassion."

St. Joseph's Church

The size of St. Joseph's (above) gives a clue to the large Hawaiian population it used to serve during the late 19th century. The church has been restored by volunteers from the local community.

Kaupō Store

The 72-year-old store sells local snacks like marlin jerky and shave ice. Opening times are erratic, but if it's closed peruse the bulletin board, plastered with business cards from all over the world.

Kaupō Gap

Driving along the rough road on the "backside" of Maui, Kaupō Gap becomes clearly visible. It was created when an erupting Haleakalā blew away a large section of the mountain's rim.

Waimoku Falls Trail

While most people head down to the Seven Pools, a trek up the Waimoku Falls Trail is a glorious experience. It begins at the Ranger Station, reaches Makahiku Falls after half a mile, then continues for another mile and a half to Waimoku Falls. The route is fragrant with tropical fruit and also wends through a thick bamboo forest.

For information about the Kaupō Gap Trail see p41

🔟 Kalaupapa National Historical Park, Moloka'i

Surrounded by the Pacific on three sides, Kalaupapa is a flat, isolated peninsula at the base of sheer sea cliffs rising almost 2,000 ft. The infamy of this beautiful patch of land stems from its role as a colony for Hansen's disease (leprosy) patients in the late 19th and 20th century. Kalaupapa

was established as a national park in 1980 and is dedicated to educating visitors with regard to a disease that has been shrouded in fear for centuries.

Kalaupapa Peninsula

🌀 To visit, you must book in advance with Damien Tours. Lunch is included with the mule ride, but if you fly in, take food and water. Visitors must be at least 16 years of age.

- Map C5
- Mon–Sat but only by prior arrangement with Damien Tours: 567 6171
- National Park Service Kalaupapa National Historical Park, Box 2222, Kalaupapa, HI 96742; 567 6802.

Top 10 Sights

1. Kalaupapa Overlook
2. Kauleo Nānāhoa (Phallic Rock)
3. Kalaupapa Trail
4. Moloka'i Lighthouse
5. The Damien Monument
6. Judd Park
7. St. Philomena Church
8. Kalawao
9. Kauhakō Crater
10. Damien Tours

Kalaupapa Coast

1 Kalaupapa Overlook

Perched on one of the highest sea cliffs on Earth, the overlook provides a panoramic view *(below right)* of the Kalaupapa Peninsula from Pālā'au State Park. The five-minute walk though woods from the parking lot to the overlook is studded with informative signs.

2 Kauleo Nānāhoa (Phallic Rock)

Accessed from the Kalaupapa Overlook, a short trail from the parking lot leads to the natural rock formation, Kauleo Nānāhoa *(left)*. Literally translated as "the penis of Nānāhoa" (a legendary character and symbol of sexuality), it's believed the stone helps women become as fertile as the land.

3 Kalaupapa Trail

Sheer cliffs form the barrier that isolates the peninsula from the rest of Moloka'i. Essentially a mule trail, the path was carved into the sheer cliffs in 1886. Today, the trail from "topside" Moloka'i to Kalaupapa is used by mule riders and hikers prepared to hug the near-perpendicular cliffs.

For more on Moloka'i, see pp96–103

Moloka'i Lighthouse

Formerly one of the Pacific's most powerful beacons, the oil lamp atop this 138-ft octagonal tower (right) was first illuminated in 1909. Three keepers' dwellings were built nearby, but by 1966 the lighthouse no longer needed nightly attention, and the last keepers departed.

The Damien Monument

A Celtic cross, erected in 1893, stands in the settlement as a memorial to the world-famous Father Damien.

Judd Park

Located next to the site of the first Hansen's Disease hospital, the park is a pleasant stop-off for lunch on the Damien Tours route. The bluff provides a fabulous view overlooking Moloka'i's sheer north shore sea cliffs.

St. Philomena Church

The most stirring site on Kalaupapa is the last of several churches built on Moloka'i by Father Damien. The priest was laid to rest here, though only his right hand remains, as the rest of his body was taken back to Belgium in 1936.

Kauhakō Crater

Formed by the eruption that created the Kalaupapa peninsula, Kauhakō Crater contains a small lake. Legend has it that goddesses Pele and Hi'iaka dug for fire here and, disappointed at finding water instead, moved on to make their home on the Island of Hawai'i.

Kalawao

On the east of the peninsula, Kalawao is the original settlement. Patients later resettled in the west of Kalaupapa, nearer the trail to "topside" and close to good anchorage.

Father Damien

A Catholic missionary priest from Belgium, Father Damien de Veuster arrived at Kalaupapa in 1873 and dedicated himself to improving the lives of the sick. Having tended his patients for 10 years, he contracted the disease himself and died in 1889. The Vatican has begun the process of declaring Damien a saint.

Damien Tours

To access Kalaupapa, you must take one of the tours offered by Damien Tours. The peninsula can be reached by air, or by foot or mule along the trail from "topside" Moloka'i. Visitors must be at least 16 years old.

Kalaupapa is still home to the few former patients who have chosen to stay, so access is strictly regulated

Left **Plantation era** Right **Statehood tourist poster**

Moments in History

1 Formation of the Islands

Each of the islands in the Hawaiian archipelago is actually the top of an underwater volcano. The oldest of the seven major islands (formed some 70 million years ago) is Kaua'i; the youngest Hawai'i, where the active Kīlauea volcano adds more landmass daily. A new island, Lō'ihi, is forming far below the ocean's surface, southeast of Hawai'i.

2 Polynesian Migration

Scholars believe that Marquesan voyagers first came to Hawai'i as early as the 4th century, with Tahitians arriving later, in the 13th. It was these two great waves of migration by skilled Polynesian seafarers that first populated the Hawaiian islands.

3 Western Contact

The landing of British explorer Captain James Cook at Kealakekua Bay on the island of Hawai'i in 1778 is generally acknowledged to be the first time Hawaiians had contact with westerners. There is evidence that Spanish ships sailed into island waters in the 16th century, but there are no records of any contact being made with the islanders.

4 King Kamehameha I Unites the Islands

An accomplished warrior chief from the island of Hawai'i, Kamehameha I waged war to conquer O'ahu and Maui, then forced the island of Kaua'i to cede to his dominion. Thus the islands were unified into the Kingdom of Hawai'i in 1809.

5 Missionaries Arrive

April 19, 1820, is a momentous – some would say notorious – date, for it was on that day that the first American missionaries arrived in Hawai'i. The first group was made up of 23 New England Congregationalists, and they landed at Kailua on Hawai'i. Over the next 20 years, many more Christian missionaries would follow, taking up residence on all the major islands.

6 The Plantation Era

Beginning in the mid-1800s, the American businessmen who first set up sugar cane production on the Hawaiian islands started importing contract laborers to work the plantations. Chinese workers were followed by Portuguese, Japanese, Latin American, Korean, and Filipino immigrants. The immigration of those groups led to the diverse ethnic mix found in the islands today.

Precontact statue

Previous pages **Baldwin Beach Park, on the north shore**

Maui's Top 10

7 The Overthrow of the Hawaiian Monarchy

On January 17, 1893, Hawai'i's last Queen, Liliu'okalani, was forcefully removed from her throne and placed under house arrest in 'Iolani Palace. The coup was the work of American businessmen based in Hawai'i, yet, despite this, U.S. President Grover Cleveland was unable to persuade the provisional government, led by Sanford P. Dole, to restore the monarchy.

8 Tourism

They came first by ship and then by airplane, and by the late 1950s tourists were coming in increasing numbers, seeking the warmth and exotic beauty of Hawai'i, a place within easy reach of the U.S. mainland's West Coast. Today, the islands host more than seven million visitors each year, arriving from every corner of the globe.

9 Statehood

Following several failed attempts, Hawai'i became the 50th state in the union on August 21, 1959. William F. Quinn and James K. Kealoha were sworn in as the first elected governor and lieutenant governor of the new state. The occasion is marked each year by a state holiday, Admission Day, celebrated on the third Friday in August.

10 Kaho'olawe's Sovereignty

No issue generates more debate in Hawai'i than the plight of the island of Kaho'olawe. Used by the U.S. military as a weapons range for decades, the bombing was finally stopped in 1990 after more than 10 years of protest. Kaho'olawe was then returned to the state and recognized for its cultural significance in 1993.

Influential Leaders

1 Kahekili
A Maui *ali'i* (chief), recognized as the most powerful – some say fierce – Hawaiian of the 1780s.

2 King Kamehameha I
The *ali'i* who succeeded in defeating Kahekili and uniting the islands into the Kingdom of Hawai'i.

3 Queen Ka'ahumanu
Born in Hāna, this favorite wife of King Kamehameha I is unrivaled in Hawai'i's feminist history.

4 Queen Liliu'okalani
Hawai'i's last and one of its most beloved monarchs, her government was overthrown in 1893.

5 Loren Thurston/ Sanford Dole
The leaders of the "Bayonet Revolution," responsible for ending the monarchy in Hawai'i.

6 Alexander & Baldwin
Samuel Alexander and Henry P. Baldwin's historic 1869 sugar plantation partnership grew into one of Hawai'i's largest companies.

7 William F. Quinn
The first elected governor of the state of Hawai'i, sworn in on August 21, 1959.

8 George Helm
Hawaiian activist and renowned musician, lost at sea with friend Kimo Mitchell in 1977 on their way to Kaho'olawe for a protest.

9 John Waihe'e
The first governor of Hawaiian ancestry, he led the state from 1986 to 1990.

10 Nainoa Thompson
The navigator for the Polynesian Voyaging Society, he has led the revival of traditional voyaging arts.

Left **Hula dancers from the 1940s** Right **Chinese Lion dance**

🔟 Music and Dance Styles

1 Hula Kahiko
In this famous art form, hula dancers are accompanied by percussive instruments made from natural materials and the intonations of one or more chanters. Ancient hula began, it is believed, as a male preserve and as religious ritual.

Slack-key guitar playing

2 Traditional Hawaiian Chant
As an oral tradition, Hawaiian stories and family histories were related through chant (oli). Ranging greatly in style, oli are used for scores of reasons, from prayers and lamentations to requests for permission to gather flora.

3 Hula 'Auana
When the practice of hula was revived during the reign of the Merrie Monarch, King David Kalākaua, a new dance style took center stage. Known as hula 'auana (modern hula), it is accompanied by instruments like the 'ukulele, guitar, standing bass, and singing voices. It is more flowing in style than hula kahiko, and dancers generally wear western clothes.

4 Slack-Key Guitar
The term slack-key refers to a style of playing the guitar in which the strings are loosened, producing a jangly sound. Gabby Pahinui was, perhaps, the most famous of Hawai'i's slack-key masters – others included Raymond Kane and Sonny Chillingworth.

5 Steel Guitar
The Hawaiian steel guitar was born in the islands around the turn of the 20th century, but exactly where, when, and how is still a point of discussion. The guitar is held horizontally on the player's lap, and a sliding steel bar is used instead of fingers on the fret board. The sound was particularly big during the Sweet Leilani era.

6 The Sweet Leilani Era
From 1900 to the early 1930s was the era when U.S. mainland composers were greatly influenced by Hawai'i, mostly as a result of the way the islands were portrayed by Hollywood. This era – when songs like Sweet Leilani, Yacka Hula Hickey Dula, and My Honolulu Lady

Hula dancers

were composed – is called the *Hapa-Haole* or Sweet Leilani era.

7 Contemporary Hawaiian Music

The modern renaissance of the Hawaiian culture, which began in the late 1960s, continues to this day, with music playing a major role. The Brothers Cazimero, Ho'okena, the late Israel Kamakawiwo'ole, and Maui's own Keali'i Reichel have combined their astounding voices with modern instruments and classic Hawaiian poetic techniques to create a magnificent new sound.

8 O-Bon

O-Bon is a traditional Japanese religious observance but has evolved, as have so many cultural practices in the islands, into a more secular event. O-Bon dances honor deceased ancestors and are joyous occasions marked by drums, music, dances, and, nowadays festival foods and fun activities.

9 Lion Dance

During February's Chinese New Year celebrations, the Lion Dance is performed all over Hawai'i. Acrobatic dancers don a lion costume and perform a dance to a steady – and very loud – drum beat designed to ward off evil and spread good fortune. Spectators fill red and gold envelopes with dollar bills and feed them to the lion to ensure future prosperity.

10 World Beat

As a miscellany of musical styles from around the world has made its way to the islands, so it is increasingly influencing musicians. Jawaiian describes a blend of reggae and Hawaiian music, and island rappers are now putting their own slant on hip-hop music.

Hawaiian Music and Dance Essentials

1 Pahu
Perhaps the most sacred of hula implements, *pahu* are drums, traditionally made using coconut tree trunk with a covering of sharkskin.

2 Ipu
A hollowed-out gourd that, in skilled hands, is used to keep the beat in hula.

3 'Ili'ili
Smooth stones – two are held in each hand and played by hula dancers in a style similar to Spanish castanets.

4 Pū'ili
Bamboo sticks, one end of each cut into a fringe so that they produce a rattling sound when played by hula dancers.

5 Kāla'au
Pairs of sticks of varying length that are struck against each other during dancing.

6 'Uli'uli
Gourd shakers that are filled with seeds and usually topped with feathers.

7 'Ukulele
A gift from the Portuguese that's now integral to modern Hawaiian music. "Jumping flea" was how Hawaiians first described the sound.

8 Guitar
Whether slack-key, steel, acoustic, or electric, the guitar is essential to Hawaiian music.

9 Standing Bass
As in jazz ensembles, the standing bass has found its way into a lot of contemporary Hawaiian music.

10 Falsetto Voice
Most easily described as male vocalists singing above their regular range, there is nothing so sweet as the sound of the Hawaiian falsetto.

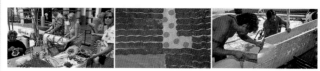

Left **Crafts stall** Center **Quilt pattern** Right **Canoe building**

Craft Traditions

1 Weaving
Traditionally, women are the weavers in Hawai'i, and many of the old everyday objects they created from *lau hala* (leaves of the pandanus tree) and the minutely thin *makaloa* (sedge grass) are considered works of art today. *Lau hala* mats, hats, and handbags are easily found in craft shops, but *makaloa* is now something of a rarity.

Coconut frond hat

2 Lei Making
There's no more enduring symbol of Hawai'i than the *lei* (garland). In the past, permanent *lei* were made from shells, seeds, bone, and feathers, and temporary *lei* from vines and leaves. Today, colorful and fragrant flowers like plumeria and tuberose are most associated with this craft.

3 Featherwork
Cloaks, *lei*, headware, and *kāhili* (standards) for the *ali'i* (chief) were all once fashioned from feathers. The birds were trapped so that specific feathers could be plucked, and then the creatures were released. Yellow, red, and black were the colors most often used. Today, artisans still craft *lei* of feathers from pheasant and other introduced species.

Lei making

4 Kapa
Used throughout old Polynesia for clothing, blankets, and decoration, Hawaiian *kapa* is made from the bark of the *wauke*, or paper mulberry tree. The process, which is restricted to women, involves pounding the bark repeatedly into paper-thin sheets that are then decorated using plant dyes and bamboo tools.

5 Stonework
Stones are an important part of Hawaiian cultural life, used in practical situations (such as building) and for spiritual needs (such as the fertility and birthing stones found on all the islands). Because stones are so highly regarded, visitors are asked not to remove them from their habitat.

6 Fishing Nets
Olonā fiber, derived from a native shrub, was commonly used in the old days to make fishing nets (a practice performed by men only). Strong and durable though it was, man-made materials such as nylon replaced *olonā* in the 20th century.

7 Canoe Building
As in all Hawaiian cultural practices, there is much ritual surrounding the building of a canoe, another of the

'Ukulele fabrication

men's arts. Traditionally, canoes are made of *koa* and always from one log, carefully selected by the boat builder. The craft is still very much alive today.

'Ukulele Making
A Portuguese import of the late 19th century, the 'ukulele quickly found its place in Hawaiian music. 'Ukulele making is still a respected art in Hawai'i, and companies like Kamaka on O'ahu and Mele 'Ukulele on Maui produce high-quality, hand-crafted instruments.

Hula Implements
The implements used by hula dancers and their accompanying chanters have changed little over hundreds of years. Though some enthusiasts still craft their own implements, hula supply shops on all the islands now allow dancers with busy 21st-century lives to purchase many of the items needed (though the materials used may not always be traditional these days).

Quilting
Among the many traditions brought by the missionaries was quilting. Not surprisingly, Hawaiian women took to the art form and made it their own, replacing New England designs with gorgeous renderings of local flora and fauna.

Lei Styles

1 Haku
Flowers, leaves, or fruit are braided onto three strands of *ti* or other natural fiber. *Haku lei* are most often worn around the head or on a hat.

2 Hili
Hili are braided *lei* made from a single plant material such as *ti* leaf or *maile*.

3 Humupapa
Flowers are sewn onto plant material such as dried banana leaves, or *lau hala*.

4 Kui
Today's most familiar *lei* – flowers strung together with needle and thread.

5 Kīpu'u
Short lengths of vines or long-stemmed leaves are knotted together.

6 Wili
Plant materials are attached to a natural backing by winding fiber around them. *Wili lei* have no knots until the very end.

7 Lei Hulu (Feather Lei)
Traditionally made of feathers from now mostly extinct or endangered native birds, the art continues using feathers from common birds.

8 Lei Pūpū (Shell Lei)
These range from *puka-shell lei*, wildly popular in the 1970s, to museum-quality *Ni'ihau-shell lei*, worth many thousands of dollars.

9 Seed Lei
Simple, single-stranded Job's Tears and intricately crafted *wiliwili-seed lei* are popular examples of this type.

10 Contemporary Lei
From silk and ribbon to yarn, currency, and even candy, contemporary *lei* are made for every occasion.

Left **Canoe festival** Right **Rodeo**

TOP 10 Festivals

1 O-Bon Festivals
You should try to get to at least one of these glorious celebrations, held between late June and early September. An Asian tradition honoring deceased ancestors, O-Bon festivals are no longer strictly religious in nature, and all are welcome at the nighttime dances, which are held at *Hongwanji*, or Buddhist missions, such as Jodo *(see p9)*.

O-Bon festival

2 A Taste of Lahaina
Maui's largest culinary festival is held each year on the Friday and Saturday closest to September 15th. Dozens of island restaurants and hotels put their best culinary creations forward while many of Hawai'i's finest modern musicians provide the entertainment.

3 Lei Day
"May Day is Lei Day in Hawai'i" say the lyrics of a popular Hawaiian song. Not that anyone in the islands needs an excuse to make, wear, or give a *lei*, but May 1st is the day Hawai'i's master *lei* makers demonstrate their amazing skills to the public.

Taro festival

4 International Festival of Canoes
For two weeks every May, master canoe builders from Polynesia and Hawai'i gather in Lahaina to celebrate their craft and the art of traditional Polynesian voyaging. There are cultural events, including a parade, throughout the period, which culminates with the launch of a canoe, built during the festival.

5 East Maui Taro Festival
Hawai'i's most important food *(see p50)* is celebrated each spring in Hāna. The first day of the three-day event features a symposium; then there's an all-day festival of food, music, hula, arts, and crafts; and finally a taro pancake breakfast.

6 Aloha Festivals
Contemporary Hawai'i is celebrated from mid-September to mid-October every year. The festivities begin on O'ahu and move through the island chain with at least a week-long celebration at every stop. A "royal court" is chosen on each

island, and the festivals are marked by floral parades, concerts, and craft fairs.

7 Chinese New Year
The sound of hundreds of thousands of firecrackers, the time-honored Lion Dance (p33), and bountiful feasts of delicious and traditional foods mark Chinese New Year in the islands. The celebration takes place in early February, and you most certainly don't have to be of Chinese heritage to take part.

8 Makawao Rodeo
Surprisingly, rodeo is a popular sport in Hawai'i and nowhere more so than in the little "paniolo" town of Makawao. Held every July 4th weekend, the festivities begin with a parade through town, and two days of rodeo events are held at an arena just up the road.

9 Maui County Fair
Carnival rides, livestock, flowers, produce, extraordinary orchid displays, and, of course, lots and lots of food – all of that and some of Hawai'i's best entertainers can be found at this fair, held in central Maui every October. The fair draws almost 100,000 folks over four days.

10 Celebration of the Arts
The brainchild of respected Hawaiian cultural specialist Clifford Nae'ole, Maui's Ritz-Carlton Kapalua resort hotel (see p116) is transformed during Easter weekend into a honeypot of cultural activities. Cultural presentations and craft demonstrations are held throughout the festival. The traditional lū'au presented in a very contemporary setting celebrates Hawaiian food, music, and dance.

Festival Foods

1 Chow Fun
Wide noodles are wok-fried with bits of pork, green onion, and other vegetables and served in a paper cone.

2 Corn Dogs
Corn-batter-coated, deep-fried hot dogs on a stick – not for the faint of heart!

3 Shave Ice
Blocks of ice ground up to the consistency of "snow" are doused with sticky syrup in any imaginable flavor and served in paper cones.

4 Malasadas
Delicious Portuguese fried donuts – without the hole – are coated with sugar and served hot.

5 Hawaiian Plate
Kālua pork, lomilomi salmon, chicken long rice, laualua, rice, poi, or any variation make up the modern Hawaiian plate.

6 Boiled Peanuts
Not just a Southern U.S. "thang," this deliciously messy treat can be found at every local festival and market.

7 Maui Hot Dogs
Bright red in color – don't ask what's in them – these are beloved on the island.

8 Spam Musubi
A big rectangle of sushi rice, a slice of grilled – or fried – Spam, all wrapped up in a piece of nori (dried seaweed). Surprisingly tasty.

9 Ice Cream
You can't have a festival without ice cream, and on Maui it's Roselani, Maui's very own producer.

10 Cotton Candy
Yes, even in paradise, this old-fashioned spun sugar treat is a hit with kids of all ages.

Left **Mt. Haleakalā lava flow** Right **La Pérouse Bay**

TOP 10 Natural Features, Gardens, and Nature Parks

Kepaniwai Park, in 'Īao Valley State Park

Pu'u Kukui (West Maui Mountains)

Atop the summit of Pu'u Kukui (Hill of Light) is one of Hawai'i's richest biological regions and the site of some of the state's last stands of pristine native rain forest. Access to the preserve here is so limited that each year a lottery is held to select just 12 lucky visitors. (See p65.)

'Īao Valley State Park

The site of Maui's bloodiest ancient battle, 'Īao Valley is sacred to Hawaiians. Within the valley stands the towering basalt pillar known as the 'Īao Needle, and Kepaniwai Park. The latter's orderly horticulture and pavilions reflect the cultures that make up modern Hawai'i. (See pp10–11.)

Pu'uōla'i, La Pérouse Bay

This 360-ft tall, red-hued cinder cone is a prominent feature at La Pérouse Bay (see p81), its form the result of Haleakalā's last eruption over 200 years ago. The coastline here had previously been the site of a thriving community. ◈ Map E6

Molokini

This crescent-shaped, partially submerged volcanic crater lies midway between Maui and Kaho'olawe. It is a marine conservation area, and its waters teem with colorful fish. (For information on trips to Molokini, see p16.)

Kaho'olawe

Currently uninhabited, Kaho'olawe is an arid island visible off South Maui. Though sacred to ancient Hawaiians, it was used as a U.S. naval bombing range for 50 years and was returned to Hawai'i in 1993. Kaho'olawe is now used only for native Hawaiian cultural and spiritual practices, and is undergoing environmental restoration (see p17).

Haleakalā National Park

The park encompasses everything from the summit of Haleakalā at 10,023 ft down to 'Ohe'o Gulch. Its massive crater was formed by water erosion. Crisscrossed by trails, dotted with cinder cones, and inhabited by rare and endangered plants and animals, this dormant volcano provides an awesome natural experience. (See pp20–21.)

Ke'anae Arboretum

Polipoli Springs State Recreation Area

High up in the cool mist of the Kula Forest Reserve on the western slope of Haleakalā is this serene area. Best known for its redwood forest, a network of trails winds through the tall trees at Polipoli. ◈ *Top of the Waipoli Road • Map G5*

Ke'anae Arboretum

Along the road to Hāna (pp22–3), the arboretum's well-marked paths thread through dense, exotic plants. The Polynesian section features Hawaiian food plants such as taro, breadfruit, and banana, and canoe plant, most important to the Pacific voyagers who migrated to Hawai'i. ◈ *Map J3 • Open daily • Free*

Wai'ānapanapa

An extraordinary sight, this fine black sand beach was formed by lava flowing into the ocean and shattering on contact with the cool water. The beach lines the edge of a cove surrounded by craggy lava peaks and lush tropical greenery. ◈ *Map L4*

Kīpahulu District

The Kīpahulu District of Haleakalā National Park was established in 1969 to protect the endangered plants and birds in its rain forest. Hiking trails among the lush foliage, vibrant flowers, and fragrant ginger lead to towering waterfalls and cool freshwater pools. ◈ *Map K5 • Kīpahulu Ranger Station: 248 7375*

Wai'ānapanapa's black sand beach

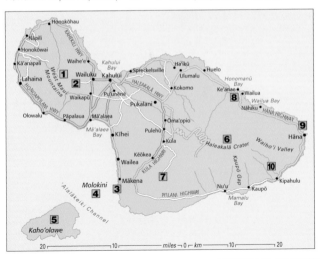

Left **'Ïao Valley Trail** Center **Haleakalā National Park** Right **Waimoku Falls**

Hikes and Trails

Waihe'e Valley Ridge Trail

Panoramic views of Central Maui and Kahakuloa await at the top of this 3-mile, moderately difficult trail through a guava grove and native scrub forest. ✪ *From Kahekili Highway (340), take Maluhia Road and after a mile look for a sign marking the trail head • Map D2*

'Ïao Valley Trail

This is a great walk for the family with well-maintained, paved paths, and easy to reach pools. Climb the steps to the top of the path for a better view of the 'Ïao Needle. Allow at least an hour and a half to explore all the park's trails. ✪ *In 'Ïao Valley State Park (see pp10–11)• Map D3*

Hoapili Trail (King's Trail)

A rather difficult hike that follows Maui's southern coastline through rugged lava fields for 6 miles, passing archaeological sites. Be sure to bring plenty of water and plan to spend about six hours if you want to hike the entire trail. ✪ *Drive to the end of Mākena Road and park on the ocean side; a white sign nearby marks the trail • Map F6*

Waikomo'i Reserve

This sanctuary for many rare and endangered Hawaiian plants and animals includes koa and 'ōhi'a trees, and forest birds such as the pueo (Hawaian owl). ✪ *Hikes begin from Haleakalā National Park (see pp20–21); reservations are required: 572 4459 • Map J3*

Waihou Spring Trail

A moderately difficult and hilly mile-long trail that takes about an hour to hike. The trail follows the Waihou Springs Forest Reserve tree plantation road, heading south to a gulch below. ✪ *Waihou Springs Forest Reserve gate on Olinda Road • Map H4*

Redwood Trail

The trail meanders from Polipoli Springs State Park through stands of redwood trees. About 2 miles long, this moderately difficult trail begins at the 6,200-ft elevation and is a part of a network of three trails: Haleakalā Ridge, Plum Trail, and Redwood Trail. ✪ *Polipoli Springs State Park • Map G5*

Haleakalā National Park

There are two trails that begin in the summit area. Sliding Sands

Ïao Valley Trail

Wai'ānapanapa beach trail

takes about half a day, descending to the valley floor before returning to the peak. Halemau'u Trail is a more difficult hike: the first mile gradually descends through shrub land to the valley rim, then 2 miles of switchbacks descend 1,400 ft to the valley floor. Both trails join up after about 9 miles. ⊗ Map J5

Wai'ānapanapa Beach Trail
Easy beach trail hikes (1–4 miles long), with spires of black lava, caves, freshwater pools, and archaeological sites to explore.
⊗ Parking, picnic tables, barbecue pits, and restrooms on site • Map L4

Waimoku Falls Trail
A 4-mile hike that takes about two hours, beginning at the Kīpahulu Visitor Center of Haleakalā National Park (the Ranger's Station) and climbing through tropical rain forest and a dense bamboo forest to the 400-ft Waimoku Falls. The trail is maintained but can be muddy. ⊗ Kīpahulu Visitor Center • 9am–5pm • 248 7375 • Map K5

Kaupō Trail
Kaupō Trail is a long and rough trek that starts at the east end of Haleakalā crater and follows along the park boundary across private ranchland. The steep and rocky trail descends through rain forest to the isolated town of Kaupō. It is a challenging hike, recommended for advanced hikers only; most hike only one way and have transportation waiting in Kaupō. ⊗ Map J5

Things to Take

1 Water
Be sure to carry plenty of drinking water as freshwater streams and pools usually contain parasites.

2 Sturdy Shoes
Lava is brittle and sharp and will tear your soles, so strong shoes with good traction are recommended.

3 Warm Clothes and Rain Gear
The weather can change quickly, so be prepared for wet and/or cold conditions.

4 Hat
A hat with a brim will protect your head from sunburn.

5 Sunscreen
The tropical sun is strong, so the frequent application of sunscreen is essential.

6 Insect Repellent
Mosquitoes and other biting critters have found their way here, so insect repellent is a good idea, especially in shady, damp areas.

7 Snacks
Food is not always available near trails, so take some fruit and sweet snacks.

8 Trash Bag
So as not to mar the pristine beauty of the island or damage its delicate ecosystems, take a plastic bag for your trash.

9 Trail Map
Maps for trails are often available at park headquarters. Review them so you are sure of your route and how long it should take. Do not stray from marked trails as you may damage the landscape.

10 Cell Phone
Always a good idea in case of an emergency, although service may be limited or unavailable in some areas.

Left **Nāpili Bay** Center **Baldwin** Right **Keālia**

🔟 Beaches

1 Kā'anapali Beach

This beautiful white sand beach fronts the Hyatt Regency Maui on one end and the Sheraton Maui at the other. Clean and safe, the beach is good for most water sports, including snorkelling and scuba diving. It's also the best beach on Maui for "beautiful people watching" – the section in front of Whalers Village is popularly known as "Dig Me." ⊗ *Map B2*

2 Nāpili Bay

A small, tranquil bay with a white sand beach that's good for swimming and safe for children. It's also right by the the Nāpili Kai Beach Resort, and there's no better place for a cocktail to accompany the sunset. ⊗ *Map C2*

3 Kapalua Bay

This gorgeous crescent of a white sand beach perennially shows up on lists of the world's best beaches. A short walk from public parking, you can rent snorkel gear, go for a catamaran ride, take a leisurely swim, or just relax in the sun. Even the humpback whales love it and in winter often frolic offshore. ⊗ *Map C1*

4 Baldwin

Just off the Hāna Highway between Kahului and Pā'ia, the water here can be a bit rough at times, and it does tend to get windy by mid-morning. But if you're an early morning person, Baldwin is lovely. ⊗ *Map F2*

5 Keālia

One of the most serene of the south shore beaches, Keālia fronts a little beach plaza of shops. It's a good place for beginners to try out their surfing or windsurfing skills, but if water sports are not your cup of tea, relax in the sun and then duck into a nearby restaurant for a frosty cocktail instead. ⊗ *Map E4*

6 Kama'ole I, II, III

If you're looking for white sand, a little shade, lifeguards, volleyball nets, picnic tables, restrooms, and showers – in other words, all the amenities of a beach park – these are the beaches for you. They are places for weekend family beach parties or barbecues. Although they are often referred to as Kam I, II, and III, Hawaiian language speakers prefer the use of their full and proper names. ⊗ *Map E5*

Kā'anapali Beach

Share your travel recommendations on traveldk.com

Kama'ole

7 Keawakapu

Keawakapu has it all: good swimming and body boarding, a nice sandy bottom, a great view of Kaho'olawe – even a parking lot. The border beach between Kīhei and Wailea, there are plenty of shallow spots, safe for even the youngest children. ◈ Map E5

8 Wailea Beach

A series of enticing white sand crescents fronting the hotels of the Wailea Resort area. Because the individual areas are bordered by lava rock outcroppings, there's almost no wave action at the edges of these beaches, making for excellent swimming and often very good snorkeling too. ◈ Map E5

9 Malu'aka

Fronting the Maui Prince Hotel, this is a wide beach, the Mākena end of which is quite sheltered (malu means sheltered in Hawaiian) and safe for small children. Just above the beach at that same end is a wonderful, grassy picnic spot. Great for a swim after visiting nearby Keawala'i Church (see p80). ◈ Map E5

10 Hāmoa

Once described by Mark Twain as the most beautiful beach on earth, this is the Hawai'i of the travel posters. Early mornings and late afternoons are the best times for swimming, for this is Maui's windward coast and the water is often rough, the waves big. So, if it looks a little wild, spread out your blanket and watch the local kids surf, body-surf, and boogie board. ◈ Map L5

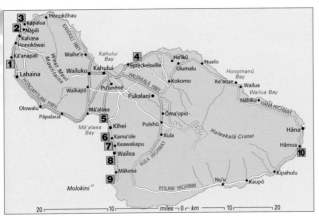

Left **Kanahā Beach Park** Right **Snorkeling**

TOP 10 Watersports Beaches

Surfing the big waves

surf is normally gentle, but it is consistent. There is no sign or parking lot; just pull off the highway where you see all the other cars. Be sure not to sit on or touch the coral.
◉ *Mile Marker 14 on Highway 30 from Lahaina* • *Map C4* • *Surfing & snorkeling*

Keka'a
1 Fronting the Sheraton Maui, you can reach this spot on Kā'anapali Beach via several different access points. Marked by a lava rock cliff, it's especially good for snorkeling. The water is clear and there is an abundance of marine life among the underwater outcroppings. It's easy to get in the water from the beach, and there are lots of places to rent gear nearby.
◉ *Map B2* • *Snorkeling*

Awalua
2 At Awalua Beach the gentle offshore waves are a good place for first-time surfers to learn the sport. The bottom descends in a slight incline out to deeper waters. ◉ *5 miles south of Lahaina on Highway 30* • *Map C3* • *Surfing*

Olowalu
3 Although it's not wide, this beach offers easy shoreline access to good snorkeling around coral heads in shallow water. There are lots of turtles and plenty of colorful reef fish. The

Mai Poina 'Oe Ia'u Beach
4 At the entrance to Kīhei, the south end of this long, narrow sand beach is popular with windsurfers; children play on the north end. And in winter it's a great spot for watching the humpback whales that migrate to Maui's warm waters. ◉ *Map E4* • *Windsurfing*

Mākena
5 The great shore break at sparkling white Oneloa (Big Beach) makes it an exciting place for body surfing and boogie boarding. On the other side of Pu'uōla'i, the cinder cone that separates Oneloa from so-called Little Beach, the waves are equally good. ◉ *Map E5* • *Body surfing & boogie boarding*

Diving among turtles

Windsurfing

Mākena Landing

A popular and often crowded launch spot for swimmers, kayakers, and scuba divers. Marine life abounds and diving visibility is good in the clear waters just outside the bay. There is a boat landing here along with a small beach and a grassy area for picnicking. ⚲ Map E5 • Kayaking & diving

Molokini

The waters inside the crescent of this underwater volcanic crater have visibility to 100 ft and are teeming with tropical fish of all shapes, sizes, and hues. There's lots of reef life, too, such as coral, pencil urchins, and sea cucumbers. The water becomes shallow near the walls of the submerged crater, and schools of triggerfish, parrot fish, and tangs swim happily around snorkelers. A sheer drop-off outside the crater walls is excellent for scuba exploration. ⚲ Access by boat only • Snorkeling & diving

Kanahā Beach Park

Great for windsurfers of all skill levels, there's a big grassy area for rigging up, and it's easy to launch from the beach. There's almost always a stiff breeze that heads inland, blowing you back to shore. Because of Kanahā's consistent winds and warm weather, many windsurfing schools give lessons here. ⚲ Map E2 • Windsurfing

Hoʻokipa Beach Park

About 10 minutes past Pāʻia on Hāna Highway, this is a beach only for experienced surfing and windsurfing enthusiasts. The beach's east side is especially popular with surfers. Kite boarders also take advantage of the constant winds and wave conditions here. ⚲ Map G2 • Surfing, windsurfing & kiteboarding

Hāna Beach County Park

Just south of Hāna town, this 700-ft-long brown sand beach is protected by a lava point, the ruins of a landing, and a pier. The bay's waters are calm, making it safe and extremely enjoyable for swimming. ⚲ Map L4 • Swimming

45

Left **Kāʻanapali Course** Right **Kapalua Bay Course**

🔟 Golf Courses

1 Kāʻanapali Royal Course
The "grand old lady" of Maui's resort courses, this 6,693-yd, par 71 course has hosted numerous PGA, LPGA, and Seniors PGA tournaments since 1963. A tip: the course is designed to be played in the wind, so expect to feel 5–15 mph tradewinds from the northeast. 🔊 2290 Kā ʻanapali Pkwy • 661 3691 • Map B2

Kapalua Plantation Course

2 Kapalua Plantation Course
Home of the prestigious Mercedes Championship since 1999, many consider this to be Hawaiʻi's best. Players on the challenging 7,411-yd, par 73 course are rewarded with some of the most spectacular scenery on Maui. The world's best have played here (including Tiger Woods), and no doubt many a round gets talked over in the course's wonderful Plantation House Restaurant *(see p52).* 🔊 300 Kapalua Drive • 669 8044 • Map C1

The Dunes at Maui Lani

3 Kapalua Bay Course
The most suburban of Kapalua's three courses, the key to playing this course well, according to one of the resort's vice presidents, is accuracy. There are strategically placed trees, 68 bunkers, and 8 water hazards on this 6,600-yd, par 72 course, designed by Arnold Palmer with Francis Duane. 🔊 300 Kapalua Drive • 669 8044 • Map C1

4 The Dunes at Maui Lani
Located on the isthmus that gives Maui its nickname of the Valley Isle, the Dunes layout has been frequently compared to classic British courses. Designer Robin Nelson did, in fact, travel to Scotland to study the links courses and integrated some of their features into this par 72. 1333 Maui Lani Parkway, Kahului • 873 0422 • Map E3

5 Waiehu Municipal
This 6,330-yd, par 72, set in Central Maui, offers stunning views of the ocean, Puʻu Kukui,

and Haleakalā. The front nine run along the ocean, while the back nine negotiate an old sand dune. ◈ Waihe'e • 270 7400 • Map D2

Wailea Gold
This award-winning course rose to international prominence in 2001, the first year it hosted the Champions Skin Game and the extraordinary foursome of Arnold Palmer, Jack Nicklaus, Gary Player, and Hale Irwin. Many consider this championship course hallowed ground, yet it's 7,078-yd, par 72 layout is manageable, even for weekend-only duffers. ◈ www.waileagolf.com • 875 7450 • Map E5

Wailea Emerald
Designer Robert Trent Jones II refers to the Emerald's "feminine characteristics" in terms of its soft visual edges. Of course, men certainly enjoy the pleasant, almost laid-back style of this course too. Some consider the 18th hole to be peerless. And the "19th" is the beautiful SeaWatch Restaurant in the Wailea clubhouse. ◈ 875 7450 • Map E5

Wailea Blue
A course that epitomizes the game of golf in Hawai'i. Most of the hazards are natural, and golfers must contend with the wonderful distraction of spec-tacularly beautiful surroundings. The course measures 6,765 yds (par 72), with an an 18th hole rated one of the best in the U.S. ◈ 875 7450 • Map E5

Mākena Golf Course
Quick greens with lots of breaks are found at the Mākena course. There are natural fea-tures including rock walls and gullies, three practice greens, a

Wailea Blue

driving range, practice bunker, and complete pro shop. ◈ 5415 Mākena Alanui • 891 4000 • Map E5

Pukalani Country Club
The only course in Upcountry Maui, the 6,962-yd, par 72 was opened in 1978 and provides a cooler experience than Maui's other courses. Set 1200 ft up the slopes of Mt. Haleakalā, the course winds through a lovely residential community. Golfers here can see the isthmus between East and West Maui, the 'Īao Needle, and both the north and south shores. ◈ 360 Pukalani St • 572 1314 • Map F3

Left **Bicycling down from Mt. Haleakalā** Right **Horseback riding**

🔝10 Outdoor Activities

Helicopter tour

1 Lū'au
A customary activity for most visitors to Hawai'i, a lū'au is a feast of traditional foods served outdoors with Hawaiian music, singing, and hula. The buffet usually includes kālua pork, lomilomi salmon with tomatoes and Maui onion, rice, teriyaki chicken, fresh salads, and haupia (coconut pudding).

2 Hiking
From easy walks to arduous hikes, Maui has miles and miles of hiking trails that will let you explore the island's diverse terrain and climatic zones. With treks through mountains, valleys, volcanic craters, lava fields, coastal areas, rain forests, dry land forests, nature preserves, and botanical gardens, it's no wonder that hiking is one of Maui's most popular activities.

3 Bicycling
Maui has hundreds of miles of designated bikeways, and renting a bicycle is easy. Organized mountain bike tours cover the Upcountry. The most popular guided tours begin at sunrise at the summit of Haleakalā and glide down to sea level along 37 miles of curves and switchbacks on well-paved, well-traveled roads.

4 Horseback Riding
Not just an hour trudge around a meadow and back to the barn, the guided horseback riding options on Maui include ranchlands and coastlines, and a full day into Haleakalā crater.

5 Snorkeling/Scuba
Hawai'i's warm clear waters, alive with colorful fish, sea turtles, dolphins, and coral, are world-famous for snorkeling and scuba diving. The adventurous can explore lava pinnacles, tubes, and caves teeming with marine life. Beginner and certified scuba excursions leave from several beaches around the island as well as Mā'alaea and Lahaina Harbors. Equipment can be rented in shops and beach kiosks.

6 Fishing
Fishing is good all year in the waters surrounding Maui and the neighboring islands. Half- and full-day charters are available on boats leaving Mā'alaea and Lahaina Harbors. You can troll for billfish, ono, mahimahi, ahi,

and opakapaka. Lines can be cast from the rocky seawalls along the harbors and northshore beaches such as Honomanū.

Whale Watching

Maui's most famous winter visitors – the humpback whales – arrive from Alaska in December and stay through April. Many charter boats carry passengers into the channels on Maui's leeward side to experience the grace and majesty of these huge and playful gentle giants.

Kayaking

Another good way to enjoy both the marine treasures and the beautiful views from offshore. Tours and rentals are available, ranging from leisurely paddling to challenging ocean treks.

Tennis

There are about 100 courts on Maui. Public courts are available on a first come, first served basis. The courts at resorts such as Kapalua, Kā'anapali, Wailea, and Mākena are usually reserved for hotel guests.

Air Tours

Soaring above the island will give you a unique perspective of Maui and a chance to observe its yet-untouched natural areas. Take flight in a helicopter, paraglider, hang glider, or a small, fixed-wing aircraft.

Humpback whale

Equipment Rental and Things to Take

1 Bike Rental
West Maui Cycles, Lahaina (661 9005), and The Island Biker (877 7744) have excellent bikes and a range of suggested routes, including the famous ride down from Haleakalā.

2 Horseback Riding
Ironwood Ranch Riding Stables (669 4991), Pony Express (667 2200), and Mendes Ranch (871 5222) offer riding in the hills and woods.

3 Dive Equipment
Rental shops abound, but Kīhei's Maui Dive (879 3388) also charters boats to Molokini.

4 Fishing Charters
Lahaina's the place: Hinatea Sportfishing (667 7548), Luckey Strike (661 4606), or Start Me Up Sportfishing (667 2774).

5 Sailing
Paragon Sailing Charters (244 2087) and Kapaluakai (667 5980) set sail from Lahaina.

6 Kayaking
Maui Kayaks in Kīhei (874 4000) offers trips in the azure coastal waters, combining kayaking and snorkeling.

7 Tom Barefoot's Cashback Tours
Maui's oldest activity center can assist with arrangements for all manner of tours and activities (270 3999).

8 Helicopter Tours
Two companies, Blue Hawaiian (871 8844) and Sunshine Helicopters (877 3227), offer airborne tours of the island.

9 Compass
A "must have" if you plan to hike or cycle in remote areas.

10 Extra Clothes
For any activities high up the slopes of Haleakalā, you must take warm clothing.

For more information on specialty tours and activities, see p114

Left **Poi with fish** Center **Shave ice** Right **Fruit stall**

Local Dishes

1 Poi
The staple of the Hawaiian diet, *poi* is made by pounding to a paste the corm of the *taro* or *kalo* plant – a task that is strictly a male preserve. Traditional Hawaiians believe their culture to be descended from a *kalo* plant, signifying the symbolic importance of this food.

Sushi

2 Kālua Pork
The centerpiece of any *lū'au*, or feast, is the whole pig, slow-roasted *(kālua)* in an underground oven – an *imu*. The meat literally falls from the bones. The same cooking method works equally well with turkey, squash, and sweet potatoes.

3 Plate Lunch
Meat, two scoops of rice, and macaroni salad. Those are the three essential elements of the plate lunch. Sold on every street corner in Hawai'i, it represents the melding of cultures, and the meat comes in many varieties, from teriyaki beef to pork and variously prepared chicken.

4 Sushi, Sashimi, and Poke
The primary Japanese culinary influences are sashimi (sliced raw fish) and sushi (raw fish, shellfish, or vegetables, served on top of, or rolled with, rice). *Poke*, the Hawaiian for diced or chopped, is Hawai'i's version of Tahitian *poisson cru* and Latin American *ceviche*. These delicious raw fish-based dishes are available everywhere from fine dining restaurants to local supermarkets.

5 Noodles and Rice
Few meals in Hawai'i are served without rice, and those that are usually come with noodles. Indeed, noodles in hot broth with pork and green onions is a common dish for breakfast, lunch, or dinner, and leftover dinner rice often reappears as fried rice for the next day's breakfast.

6 Portuguese Sweet Bread and Bean Soup
Fresh from the oven and slathered with creamy butter is the best way to enjoy this wonderful bread, brought by Hawai'i's Portuguese immigrants. Originally baked in outdoor brick ovens, it is now available at markets throughout the islands. Every

Lū'au feast

Recommend your favorite restaurant on traveldk.com

family in Hawai'i, whether of Portuguese heritage or not, has its own Portuguese bean soup recipe. Brimming with beans, meat, and vegetables, it can be a hearty meal unto itself, especially when accompanied by a thick slice of sweet bread.

Kim Chee
Brought by Hawai'i's Korean immigrants, *kim chee* is simply pickled cabbage, but for those who love hot – that is, VERY HOT – flavors, it is a "must try." Traditionally, the cabbage is stored in tightly sealed jars and buried in the ground, then dug up as and when needed.

Tropical Fruit
Mango, papaya, guava, *liliko'i* (passion fruit), bananas, and, of course, pineapple. Pure and simple right off the tree, blended into a delicious fruit smoothie, or transformed into an amazing dessert, these are truly paradisiacal flavors.

Shave Ice
It has other names in other places – snow cone is one – but it is simply small chips of ice, flavored with one or more of myriad syrups, served in a paper cone. Cool and refreshing on a hot summer day, the rainbow variety shave ice has become a virtual symbol of Hawai'i.

Spam
Yes, it's true. One of the most maligned foods in history is one of Hawai'i's most popular and beloved. Canned Spiced Ham (SPAM) was originally known as a military staple since it's easy to keep for long periods of time. It is, perhaps, the large military presence in Hawai'i that first accounted for its curious popularity in the islands.

Local Food Stops

1 Aloha Mixed Plate
Exceptional plate lunches served outside, where there's a grand ocean view. ◈ *1285 Front St, Lahaina*

2 L & L Drive-In
A rapidly expanding chain of local fast food restaurants, popular with islanders for decades. ◈ *790 Eha, Wailuku (also in Lahaina, Kahului, Kihei)*

3 Sack 'n Save
A great place for a wide array of *poke* and other island-style specialties like pre-packed sushi. ◈ *790 Eha, Wailuku*

4 Tokyo Tei
An island institution, serving the freshest sashimi in town. ◈ *1063 L. Main St, Wailuku*

5 Home Maid Bakery
Amazing assortment of pastries and wonderful hot *malasadas* (Portuguese donuts) early morning and late at night. ◈ *1005 L. Main St, Wailuku*

6 Sam Sato's
THE place for noodles, teriyaki, and yummy local-style turnovers. ◈ *1750 Wili Pa Loop, Wailuku*

7 Takamiya Market
A local food treasure and a great place to stock up on ingredients for a picnic. ◈ *359 N. Market, Wailuku*

8 Pukalani Superette
Wide range of local dishes and the best ice cream selection. ◈ *15 Makawao Ave, Pukalani*

9 Dragon Dragon
Prawns with walnuts, whole fish, crab in black bean sauce, and lychee sherbet – all delicious. ◈ *Maui Mall, Kahului*

10 Da Kitchen
Sumo-sized portions of popular local foods – teriyaki, katsu, Hawaiian plate. ◈ *425 Koloa St, Kahului*

Left **Plantation House Restaurant** Right **Hāli'imaile General Store**

Restaurants

1 Pineapple Grill
Located within the Kapalua Resort area of West Maui, the Pineapple Grill's delicious upscale menu (using local produce where possible) is served in a relaxed environment. The gorgeous views add to the fine dining experience. *(See p69.)*

2 Pacific'O & I'O
Sister restaurants steps apart, both feature the extra-ordinarily creative cuisine of chef James McDonald with the focus on fresh fish. Both offer indoor and outdoor dining; the patios are literally on the beach, providing a picture postcard ambience. *(See p60).*

3 Roy's Kahana Bar & Grill
Hawai'i's undisputed father of East-meets-West cuisine, Roy Yamaguchi operates more than 30 restaurants throughout the islands and the mainland U.S.

Sansei Seafood Restaurant

Always bustling, with a hip and lively atmosphere. *(See p69).*

4 Sansei Seafood Restaurant & Sushi Bar
New Wave Sushi and innovative, Japanese-inspired Pacific Rim cuisine make Sansei one of the most popular restaurants in the state. The restaurant has two locations on Maui, both with laser karaoke, early and late night specials, and live music on Saturday nights. *(See p69).*

5 Plantation House Restaurant at Kapalua
The chef here, Alex Stanislaw, combines the smoky, earthy flavors of his Mediterranean heritage with local Hawaiian ingredients to create a cuisine all his own. Set above the Kapalua resort, the Plantation House Restaurant offers spectacular views. *(See p69).*

Pacific'O

6 A Saigon Café
Operating one of the most popular ethnic restaurants on Maui, owner Jennifer Nguyen claims to be too busy to put up a sign! Though this makes the place rather difficult to locate, the food is great and inexpensive. (See p74).

7 Mala, An Ocean Tavern
On the oceanfront, chef/owner Mark Ellman's newest eatery features organic ingredients where possible, small plates, and reasonable prices. The signature dessert, Carmel Miranda, is a favorite. (See p60).

8 Spago
America's best-known celebrity chef has landed on Maui. Wolfgang Puck's signature restaurant, Spago, is located in the beautiful Four Seasons Resort. Puck's now-classic California cuisine receives an island twist in a stunning setting. (See p83).

9 Mama's Fish House
A Maui institution, Mama's beach house specializes in island-style hospitality. Steps from the ocean in Ku'au, it's no wonder that fresh fish is the main event here. Mama's is known for its huge portions, home-baked bread, and mega-desserts. (See p89).

10 Hāli'imaile General Store
Upcountry Maui's best restaurant is housed in a marvelously refurbished 1925 plantation store. Chef/Owner Beverly Gannon's signature creations like Hunan Lamb, Szechuan Salmon, and Ahi Napoleon have garnered national acclaim. Save room for dessert. (See p89).

Hawaiian Foodstuffs

1 Local Greens
Small farms grow dozens of varieties of greens for Hawai'i's best restaurants.

2 Moi
Once enjoyed exclusively by ali'i (royalty), this small, delicate fish is now on menus throughout the Islands.

3 Tropical Fruit
Not just for breakfast or dessert – pineapple, papaya, guava, liliko'i, and lychee turn up in salsas and sauces.

4 Local Fishes
A myriad variety of local fishes – like mahimahi, ahi, opakapaka, onaga – form the foundation of island cuisine.

5 Moloka'i Sweet Potatoes
With their brilliant purple flesh, these wonderful potatoes add color as well as flavor to many dishes.

6 Corn (from Kahuku, Kula, Pahoa, Moloka'i)
Chefs delight in using locally grown sweet corn – both yellow and white.

7 Slipper Lobster
Smaller than their Maine cousins. The sweet tail meat is most often used in recipes.

8 Pohole
These bright green, crunchy, and delicious ferns grow in East Maui and are often served with tomatoes.

9 Local Meat
Beef, lamb, even elk and venison are produced by Hawai'i ranches and used by local chefs.

10 'Ulupalakua Strawberries
Big, red, juicy, and delicious, these strawberries grow well in the middle elevations of Mt. Haleakalā.

AROUND MAUI

MAUI'S TOP 10

Left **Front Street** Center **Pioneer Inn, Front Street** Right **Dancers at the Feast at Lele**

Lahaina

DELIGHTFUL LAHAINA *has always been a small hub of activity on Maui. In its 19th-century heyday, it was first the royal capital of the entire Hawaiian Kingdom, then an important port for Pacific whaling ships. Christian missionaries clashed with bawdy sailors here, before the lure of sugar turned it into a thriving plantation town. Now something of a tourist hot spot, Lahaina is filled with shops, galleries, restaurants, bars, and historic sights, while the rainbow-crowned Pu'u Kukui (West Maui Mountains) provide a magnificent backdrop.*

Left **Maria Lanakila Church** Right **Banyan Tree**

🔟 Sights

1. Front Street
2. Wo Hing Temple
3. Master's Reading Room
4. Hale Pa'ahao
5. Waiola Church
6. Waine'e Cemetery
7. Maria Lanakila Church
8. Hale Pa'i
9. Sugar Cane Train
10. Jodo Mission

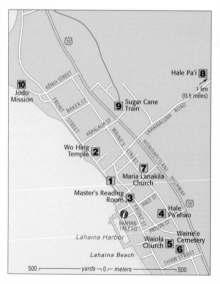

Previous pages **Garden of Eden Arboretum, East Maui**

Lahaina Harbor

leave the employment of others and set up their own businesses. The Wing Ho Temple, built by a Chinese fraternal society as a social hall, now preserves the history and contributions of Maui's Chinese community through its exhibits. ✆ *10am–4pm daily • Donation*

Front Street

This oceanfront thoroughfare is Lahaina's main street. Lined with all the trappings of a vacation town, from souvenir shops and activity reservation outlets to a plethora of bars and restaurants, Front Street bustles day and night. It is the site of major festivals throughout the year (A Taste of Lahaina in September, Halloween's Mardi Gras of the Pacific in October, the International Festival of Canoes in May) and a continual stream of smaller events, including the weekly Friday Night is Art Night. *(See pp8–9.)*

Wo Hing Temple

This brightly painted building illustrates the influence of Chinese immigrants to the commerce of Maui. Brought in great numbers to work on sugar plantations, it was not long before the Chinese settlers had enough money to

Master's Reading Room

A beautifully preserved coral and fieldstone building. Its exterior hasn't changed a jot since its completion in 1834, when it was built for ships' officers and their families as a respite from the "heat and unpleasant dust of the market." It now houses the Lahaina Restoration Foundation. ✆ *Corner of Front & Dickenson streets • Access via Baldwin House, next door • 661 3262*

Hale Pa'ahao

This mid-19th century structure served as Lahaina's prison, the inmates largely made up of ship deserters, drunks, reckless horse riders, and violators of the Sabbath. Built by convicts in the 1850s from blocks of stone salvaged from the old fort, the prison had a catwalk for use by an armed guard and wooden cells to hold the criminals. ✆ *10am–4pm daily • Free*

Left **Wo Hing Temple** Right **Master's Reading Room**

For places to stay in Lahaina **see pp118–120**

Left **Waine'e Cemetery** Right **Sugar Cane Train**

Waiola Church

Immortalized by American author James Michener in his novel *Hawai'i*, this church was built in the early 1800s and dedicated in 1823. Destroyed three times – twice by windstorms and once by fire – the building was repositioned during its last reconstruction in 1951 and has been standing sturdily since. Still known largely as Waine'e Church, it was officially renamed Waiola ("water of life") in 1953.

Waine'e Cemetery

The first Christian cemetery in Hawai'i. Many Hawaiian *ali'i* (royals) are buried here, including King Kaumuali'i, the last king of Kaua'i; Queen Keōpūolani, the highest Hawaiian *ali'i* ever baptized as a Protestant; and Princess Nahienaena, sister of Kings Kamehameha II and III.

Maria Lanakila Church

Although the Catholic priests who arrived on Maui in 1846 were unpopular with the established Protestant leaders, Catholicism quickly became the island's largest denomination as a result of the influx of Catholic laborers from Portugal and the Philippines. The church was built in 1856 and enlarged in 1858. The beautiful

High and Mighty

Queen Keōpūolani, one of Hawai'i's highest ranking *ali'i*, was thought to have so much *mana* (spiritual power) that she was descended from the gods. The *kapu* (restrictions) surrounding her were so complex that she lived in total isolation. No one was allowed to look at her or cross her shadow. She became a wife of Kamehameha I, and he too had to bow in her presence.

structure, which now stands at Waine'e and Dickenson streets, is a replica of the 1858 church.

Hale Pa'i

On the campus of Lahainaluna, the oldest high school west of the Rockies, this hillside building holds the history of the written word in Hawai'i. Until the mid-1800s, Hawaiian was a spoken language only. In order to spread the Bible's word, Protestant missionaries used English letters to transliterate Hawaiian, and they brought a printing press with them specifically for the task. A replica of the press and the pages it printed are displayed here. ⊘ *10am–4pm daily • Donation*

Sugar Cane Train

Railroads traversed the landscape of Hawai'i during the plantation era, with steam locomotives pulling trains that hauled sugar cane from the fields to the mills. The first of these in West Maui began operating around 1890 and continued until 1950, when it was replaced by trucks. The Lahaina Kāʻanapali & Pacific Railroad (affectionately called the Sugar Train) is an authentic reproduction of the trains that ran through the fields of West Maui, but these days it carries passengers instead of sugar. Its six-mile route runs between Lahaina and Kāʻanapali, crossing a curved wooden viaduct that offers panoramic views.

◈ Trains depart Lahaina at 11am, 1pm, 2:30pm, and 4pm daily; Thu evening dinner train departs 4:30pm • 661 0080 • Adm

Jodo Mission
10 This three-story pagoda sits at the outer edge of Lahaina town. In its courtyard stands a giant statue of Buddha, the largest outside Japan, placed in commemoration of the 1868 arrival of the first Japanese immigrants to Maui. The serene grounds are open to the public; the buildings are not.

Giant Buddha, Jodo Mission

A Lahaina Stroll

Early Morning

Lahaina is hot virtually year round, so it's best to start early in the day. Most historical spots are within a block or two of Front Street, so begin your walking tour at the south end in Maluʻuluʻolele Park (see p9), and head roughly north, in the direction of the **Kāʻanapali Beach** (see p42).

The first sites you'll encounter are **Banyan Tree Park**, the old **Lahaina Courthouse**, and **Lahaina Harbor** (see p8 for all three). Just a block farther is the **Baldwin House** (p9), the two-story, New England-style home of a Protestant missionary. The building also served as Baldwin's medical office, and the early dental equipment on display makes you feel lucky to live in this age of effective anesthetics!

Continue your stroll to the Wo Hing Temple where the influence of Chinese immigrants to Maui can be seen, along with early movies made by American inventor Thomas Edison.

Late Morning

Take a break for lunch or a cool libation at any of Front Street's oceanfront restaurants. For a quick bite, Cheeseburger in Paradise is immensely popular. Portions are big, prices small, and the ocean view, especially from upstairs, is glorious.

When you're re-energized, there are plenty of trendy boutiques, art galleries, and souvenir shops all along Front Street to attract your vacation money (see p61).

Price Categories

Price categories include a three-course meal for one, a glass of house wine, and all unavoidable extra charges including tax.

$	under $20
$$	$20–$30
$$$	$30–$45
$$$$	$45–$60
$$$$$	over $60

Pacifico'O

Places to Eat and Nightlife

1 Pacific'O & I'o
Sister restaurants with the innovative touch of James McDonald behind them. Highlights include fresh fish encrusted with coconut and macadamia nuts and a wonderful lobster salad.
® *Pacific'O, 505 Front St; 667 4341 • Pacific I'o (dinner only) 661 8422 • $$$$$*

2 The Feast at Lele
The folks behind the Old Lāhaina Lū'au designed this dinner show, featuring the music and dance of Hawai'i, Tonga, Tahiti, and Samoa. James McDonald *(see Pacific'O, above)* takes care of the Pacific Island food. ® *505 Front St. • 667 5353 • $$$$$*

3 David Paul's Island Grill
Chef David Paul Johnson creates his regularly changing menu using the freshest local ingredients. Ask to sit on the outdoor Sunset Terrace for a wonderful, unobstructed ocean view.
® *Lahaina Center • 662 3000 • $$$$$*

4 Gerard's
Gerard Reversade has been honing his own style of classic French cooking mixed with island flair for more than 20 years.
® *At the Plantation Inn, 174 Lahainaluna Rd. • 661 8939 • $$$$$*

5 'Ulalena
From the creators of Cirque du Soleil,

this extravagant production tells the story of Hawai'i's history in song, dance, and acrobatics.
® *878 Front St. • 661 9913 • $$$$*

6 Longhi's
The trademark black & white décor, open-air setting, and Italian-island fare has been part of Lahaina since 1976. ® *888 Front St. • 667 2288 • $$$$$*

7 BJ's Chicago Pizza
Enjoy delicious pizzas, great Lahaina Harbor views, and live music at this long-standing restaurant. ® *730 Front St. • 661 5390 • $*

8 Hard Rock Café
Huge burgers, messy ribs, frou-frou drinks, and plenty of rock 'n' roll memorabilia.
® *Lahaina Center • 667 7400 • $$*

9 Old Lahaina Lū'au
The Old Lahaina *Lū'au* is simply the best experience of its kind anywhere in Hawai'i. The dinner buffet is bountiful, the music and hula glorious, the setting extraordinary.
® *1251 Front Street • 667 1998 • $$$$$*

10 Mala, An Ocean Tavern
Chef Mark Ellman's latest venture is on the beach. Organic ingredients and affordable prices. ® *1307 Front St. • 667 9394 • $$$$$*

Lahaina Harbor

Around Maui – Lahaina

Left **Lahaina Scrimshaw** Center **Village Galleries** Right **Lahaina Cannery Mall**

TOP 10 Shopping

1 Maggie Coulombe Maui
This talented Canadian emigre designs fabulous women's clothing; the shop's accessories, like Moda sunglasses, handbags, and shoes are the perfect complements. ◉ *505 Front St.*

2 Lahaina Gateway
This vast shopping center in West Maui includes a huge Barnes & Noble bookstore and a Lahaina Farms grocery store. There are also specialty shops, boutiques, and restaurants. ◉ *Honoapi'ilani Hwy & Keawe St.*

3 Maui Divers
Pearls of every size, shape, and color set in rings, earrings, bracelets, and necklaces are the specialties of Maui Divers. ◉ *640 Front St. (opposite the Banyan Tree)*

4 Lahaina Scrimshaw
Since the use of whale bones and teeth was prohibited in 1973, 21st-century scrimshanders use fossilized bone or walrus tusk for their amazingly intricate creations. ◉ *845A Front St.*

5 Crazy Shirts
The king of T-shirt shops, Crazy Shirts designs are distinctive, and the shirts made of the highest quality cotton. ◉ *865 Front St. (as well as many other outlets elsewhere in Maui)*

6 The Whaler Ltd.
Extraordinary glass and a hearty trawl of nautical-themed objects fill this wonderful shop. ◉ *866 Front St.*

7 Take Home Maui
You can't leave Maui without a few sweet, juicy pineapples! This shop packs up all of Maui's best edible produce – papaya, Maui onions, coconuts, macadamia nuts – and will even deliver your order right to the airport. ◉ *121 Dickenson St.*

8 Village Galleries
Art galleries in Lahaina come and go, but Village Galleries has staying power. Lynn Shue has represented some of Maui's finest artists and continues to bring new talent into her fold. ◉ *120 Dickenson St.*

9 Lahaina Cannery Mall
In a refurbished pineapple cannery, 50 stores selling everything from aloha wear to fine art. There's a food court too, and a fun Mexican restaurant called Compadres. ◉ *Front St.*

10 Lahaina Printsellers
A long-established Maui gallery with a respected penchant for reproductions of old Hawai'i maps. ◉ *1013 Limahana Pl.*

Left **Kahakuloa Head** Center **Keka'a Beach** Right **Honolua Store**

West Maui

PU'U KUKUI (THE WEST MAUI MOUNTAINS) *dominate the interior of this side of the island; the coastal area between their rainbow-crowned peaks and the ocean is made up of sandy beaches, resorts, golf courses, and a remote scenic drive. Kā'anapali was Maui's first planned resort community, its hotels, shops, and golf courses bordering a three-mile, sparkling white sand beach. Dozens more resort complexes stretch through Honokōwai, Kahana, and Nāpili. Except for a small village, there is nothing but dramatic scenery past Kapalua, the last resort, from where the road hugs the coastline around the mountains on its way back to Wailuku.*

Left **Ono Surf Bar and Grill** Right **Kahakuloa Village**

🔟 Sights

1. Whalers Village Museum
2. Keka'a
3. Honolua Store
4. Honokahua Preservation Site
5. Maunalei Arboretum
6. Honokōhau Valley
7. Nākālele Point (Blowhole)
8. Bellstone
9. Kahakuloa Village/ Kahakuloa Head
10. Pu'u Kukui

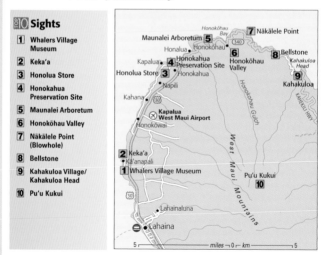

Whalers Village Museum

Whalers Village Museum

The skeleton of a 40-ft Sperm whale guards the entrance to Whalers Village, a museum that presents a vivid picture of the 19th-century Pacific whaling industry. Photo murals, an authentic whaling boat complete with gear, and a re-created ship's forecastle graphically illustrate the seafaring life. ⊗ *Map B2 • 2nd level of Whalers Village Shopping Complex • 9am–6pm daily • Free*

Keka'a

Keka'a is a *lele* (a jumping off point for spirits going to the next world). This particular one is a high bluff of black lava rock from which ancient Hawaiians believed their spirits sprung forth. It is directly in front of the Sheraton Maui on Kā'anapali Beach. Also known – some would say disrespectfully – as Black Rock, this area is one of the best snorkeling spots on Maui. It's easily accessible from the beach and teems with marine life. ⊗ *Map B2*

Honolua Store

Pineapple plantation carpenters built the Honolua Store in 1929, and it looks much the same today as it did when it first opened. Now the merchandise is a bit more upscale, and clothing here sports the Kapalua Resort butterfly logo. Breakfast, sandwiches, and local foods such as Spam musubi *(see p51)* and a variety of plate lunches are available at the deli counter. ⊗ *Map C1 • 502 Office Rd., Kapalua*

Honokahua Preservation Site

This important historical site was uncovered during the construction of a hotel. The area contains more than 900 ancient Hawaiian burials dating from 610 to 1800 A.D. So significant and sacred is this place that the hotel had to shift site slightly to accommodate it. Now carpeted with lush grass and bordered by native plants, it is recognized as a sacred Hawaiian site. ⊗ *Map C1 • On the grounds of the Ritz-Carlton Kapalua • Limited access*

Honokahua Preservation Site

For places to stay in West Maui see pp116–20

Left **Honokōhau Valley** Right **Bellstone**

Maunalei Arboretum

D.T. Fleming, one of the first managers of the pineapple plantation on West Maui, established this privately owned arboretum in 1926. Fleming traveled the world collecting plants and trees, and his search has resulted in an abundance of introduced species coexisting with the endemic plant life. Native bird species also inhabit the arboretum. ◎ *Map C1*

Honokōhau Valley

Traveling north from Honolua Bay will take you on a scenic coastal drive. Part of this is through the fecund Honokohau Valley, which positively bursts with fruit trees and lush vegetation. Wind down your window and breath in the scented air. ◎ *Map C1*

Nākālele Point (Blowhole)

This is the most northerly point on Maui and the site of Hawai'i's first lighthouse. When

Nākālele Point

Pineapple

Introduced to the islands only in the early 1800s, by the end of that century pineapple had become a vital commodity in West Maui, with 2,500 acres given over to the fruit's production. Though its economic importance dwindled in the latter part of the 20th century (when canning factories were turned into shopping malls), pineapple cultivation continues, and the fruit is still much loved on Maui today.

---

the surf is just right, sea water is forced as high as 100 ft into the air through a hole in the shoreline lava tube here. The blowhole is a short walk down the hill from the road, but be very careful because the waves and geysers are unpredictable. ◎ *Map D1*

Bellstone

This large volcanic rock, sitting on the side of the road just before Mile Marker 16 on the road past Kapalua, is so named because it sounds like a bell when struck in exactly the right spot. Use another rock or stick to gently strike the stone – it will probably take several attempts to find the right spot. By way of a hint, if you hit the rock on the side facing the mountain, it should resound with a metallic clank. ◎ *Map D1*

Kahakuloa Village/
Kahakuloa Head

For nearly 1,500 years Hawaiian families have inhabited Kahakuloa, growing *kalo (see p94)* on stone terraces and using aqueducts to irrigate the crops from mountain streams. There are no gas stations or restaurants in the village, and the most prominent building is a lovely, small church. East of the village, the monolithic 636-ft Kahakuloa Head rises majestically from the water's edge. Ⓢ *Map D1–2*

Pu'u Kukui

One of the wettest places on earth, Pu'u Kukui is the highest point in the West Maui Mountains, and also the proper name of the entire range. The region is home to more rare native plants and birds than anywhere else in Hawai'i. Inhabitants include the 'Eke Silversword, which is found only in this mountain range and wild i'iwi birds, extinct in most of the rest of the island chain. Access to this 8,600-acre private preserve is granted by the Kapalua Nature Society, which uses a lottery system to choose just 12 hikers per year. Ⓢ *Map D3 • Kapalua Resort, 800 Kapalua Dr., Kapalua • 669 0244*

Kahakuloa Village Church

An Afternoon Away from the Crowds

Early Afternoon

Head west along Route 30 from the Kā'anapali Resort area, and stock up on snacks and beverages at the quaint **Honolua Store** in Kapalua *(see p67)*.

Stop at either **D.T. Fleming Beach** or **Honolua Bay** *(p66)* for an invigorating swim in summer or the thrill of watching experienced surfers in winter. Drive carefully along narrow Route 30 from Kapalua all the way around to Wailuku. The road, barely wide enough for one car at points, twists and turns with the coastline, hugging the mountainside with sheer drop-offs to the ocean below.

Late Afternoon

After you travel through the lush Honokohau Valley, stop at **Nākālele Point** for a short hike to experience the awesome force of the blowhole. Here the vivid red-hued cliffs drop to the ocean below and trails along the bluffs offer terrific ocean views. The wide expanses of grassy bluffs are great for a picnic.

After another brief stop at Mile Marker 16 to try ringing the **Bellstone**, continue along the route through the tiny village of Kahakuloa. A few miles farther finds you at **Kaukini Gallery** *(p67)*, which displays and sells the work of local artisans.

From here you will soon return to "civilization," passing through the communities of Waihe'e and Waiehu. Continue "home" along the main highways.

Left **Nāpili Bay** Center **D.T. Fleming Beach Park** Right **Honolua Bay**

Best Beaches

1 Hanaka'ō'ō
This County Beach Park is actually the southernmost end of Kā'anapali Beach. Several canoe clubs call this beach home and host occasional paddling events. ◈ *Map B2*

2 "Dig Me"
The beach in front of Whalers Village *(see opposite)* is the portion of Kā'anapali known to locals as "Dig Me," as in "look at me, aren't I lovely?" If you'd rather look than be looked at, grab a table and a cocktail at the Barefoot Bar *(see p68)*. ◈ *Map B2*

3 Keka'a
Fronting the Sheraton Maui, this is one of the island's best snorkeling spots. Keka'a is its proper Hawaiian name, but you may also hear it referred to as Black Rock. ◈ *Map B2*

4 Airport
So-called because of its proximity to a long-gone small airport. The beach has been upgraded in recent years, and now has picnic tables and restroom facilities. ◈ *Just north of Kā'anapali • Map B2*

5 Honokōwai
Located across the road from the condos and mini-strip malls, Honokōwai Beach Park is good for snorkeling and excellent for small children who like to play at the water's edge. Lots of food and other services are only seconds away. ◈ *Map B–C2*

6 Nāpili Bay
One of the calmest and most pleasant beaches on Maui is this small, sandy crescent adjacent to the Nāpili Kai Beach Resort. The sandy bottom and calm waters are safe for even the smallest swimmers. ◈ *Map C2*

7 Kapalua Bay
This gorgeous sandy beach consistently appears on "best beaches" lists in travel magazines. It's adjacent to the Kapalua Bay Hotel, and you can rent snorkel gear right on the beach. ◈ *Map C1*

8 D. T. Fleming Beach Park
This beach on Honokōhau Bay has parking, showers, barbecues, and good swimming off a long, wide beach complete with trees for shade. But watch out in the winter months, when the surf here can get very big. ◈ *Map C1*

9 Mokulē'ia
Past Fleming with access down a dirt and rock trail, and on-the-road parking only, this is a popular winter surf spot but only for experienced wave riders. Summer swimming and snorkeling are good. ◈ *Nr. Honolua • Map C1*

10 Honolua Bay
Just past Mile Marker 32 is Honolua Bay – park as soon as you come to the dirt road. This is another good spot for experienced surfers, and during the summer months, there's good swimming and snorkeling too. ◈ *Map C1*

For all of Maui's top beaches, see pp42–45

Left **Kahana Gateway Shopping Center** Center **Nāpili Plaza** Right **Reyn's**

TOP 10 Shopping

1 Whalers Village
An all-encompassing shopping center, where you'll find every type of store imaginable from Crazy Shirts to Jessica's Gems, from the T-Shirt Factory to Cinnamon Girl, and from Coach to Louis Vuitton. ◎ *2435 Kā'anapali Parkway • Map B2*

2 Honolua Surf Co.
Even if your life is not centered on the ocean you can still look the part with board shorts, hoodies, and other casual wear. ◎ *Whalers Village (Map B2) • Lahaina Cannery (Map B3)*

3 Dolphin Galleries
A reputable outlet, specializing in jewelry and sculpture, and with some two-dimensional art as well. Any purchase can be shipped home for you. ◎ *Whalers Village (Map B2) • The Shops at Wailea (Map E5)*

4 Kahana Gateway Shopping Center
Although restaurants such as Roy's Kahana Bar & Grill *(see p69)*, Maui Brew Pub, and McDonald's dominate, there are also souvenir shops, a few casual clothes and swimwear shops, a nail salon, a bank, a laundromat, and gas station. ◎ *4405 Honoapi'ilani Hwy., Kahana • Map C2*

5 Nāpili Plaza
A neighborhood-style center, with a surprise to be found in the form of a tiny military museum.

There's also a good florist, a bank, and mail services center. ◎ *5095 Nāpilihau St., Nāpili • Map C2*

6 Maui Hands
This gallery displays the work of some of the island's finest artists. Offerings include hand-blown glass, Hawaiian woodwork, handpainted clothing, and decorative basketry. ◎ *Hyatt Regency Hotel, Ka'anapali Beach Resort • Map B2 • 667 7997*

7 Totally Hawaiian Gift Gallery
A wide variety of island arts and crafts, including Niiahu shell jewelry, perfumes, quilts, and dolls. ◎ *Whalers Village • Map B2 • 667 4070*

8 Reyn's
Best known for the "inside-out" aloha shirts sported by every businessman in the state, Reyn's also makes great women's wear. ◎ *Whalers Village • Map B2 • 661 9032*

9 Honolua Store
A creaking old general store, where the groceries and sundries share space with a deli counter, and the front room has high-end clothing, books, and gifts. ◎ *502 Office Rd., Kapalua • Map C1 • 665 9105*

10 Kaukini Gallery
An attractive gallery, filled with a variety of locally made art and craft items, and a welcome stop on the challenging road around Kahakuloa Head. ◎ *Outside Kahakuloa village • Map D2 • 244 3371*

Left **Barefoot Bar** Right **'OnO Surf Bar & Grill**

ⓉⓄⓅ10 Bars & Clubs

1 Cascades Bar & Lounge
Snack on sushi and sip on a sake or a Blue Hawai'i amid the glow of tiki torches. Classic tropical setting with palm trees and a beautiful ocean vista. ◎ *Hyatt Regency Maui • 661 1234 • Map B2*

2 Don The Beachcomber Tiki Lounge
Enjoy an original Mai Tai along with island-style *pūpū* (appetizers) amidst the retro-Polynesian atmosphere of this bar. ◎ *Royal Lahaina Resort • 661 3611 • Map B2*

3 'OnO Surf Bar & Grill
This pleasant, casual poolside spot offers all-day dining, including a breakfast buffet, and is transformed at sunset with the addition of live entertainment. Naturally, the views are captivating too. ◎ *At the Westin Maui • 667 2525 • Map B2*

4 Barefoot Bar
You can't get closer to the beach than this, a bar where you can wiggle your toes in the sand. One of the island's best for cocktails, appetizers, sunset, and checking out the beautiful people on "Dig Me" Beach. ◎ *At Hula Grill • 667 6636 • Map B2*

5 Leilani's on the Beach
Renowned for fantastic ice cream drinks – there's a full bar, too, of course – and great *pūpū* (appetizers), Leilani's is also just a few steps across the sand from "Dig Me" Beach. ◎ *At Whalers Village • 661 4495 • Map B2*

6 Lagoon Bar
Through the lush gardens and across the wooden bridge to the Lagoon Bar for a light lunch or, in the evening, a truly amazing event: the nightly Torch Lighting and Cliff Diving. ◎ *At the Sheraton Maui • 661 0031 • Map B2*

7 Maui Brewing Co.
Maui's only brewpub is a favorite hangout of west side residents who enjoy the nightly live music. The wine list has received the Award of Excellence for three years running. The beer is brewed in three large copper vats which can be seen by the patrons. ◎ *Kahana Gateway Center • 669 3474 • Map C2*

8 Sea House Restaurant
Right on the ocean at Napili Kai Beach Resort, this is one of the best places for watching the sunset. ◎ *5900 Honoapi'ilani Hwy, Napili • 669 1500 • Map B2*

9 Kupanaha
Great for the whole family, this evening of dinner, magic, and illusions is based on the story of the Hawaiian goddess Pele and features hula and chant. ◎ *Kā'anapali Beach Hotel • 661 0011 • Map B2*

10 Alaloa Lounge
The panoramic views of the Pacific and nearby islands make this the perfect spot to sip a cocktail. ◎ *At the Ritz Carlton, Kapalua • 669 6200 • Map C1*

Pineapple Grill

Price Categories

Price categories include a three-course meal for one, a glass of house wine, and all unavoidable extra charges including tax.

$	under $20
$$	$20–$30
$$$	$30–$45
$$$$	$45–$60
$$$$$	over $60

🏆10 Places to Eat

1 Tiki Terrace Restaurant
This open-air restaurant is the perfect showcase for Chef Tom Muromoto's unique style of Hawai'i's regional cuisine. It is one of the only places on Maui to sample authentic Hawaiian dishes. ◈ *Kā'anapali Beach Hotel, 2525 Kā'anapali Parkway • 661 0011 • Map B2 • $$$*

2 Hula Grill
This fabulous reproduction of a kama'āina beach house will transport you back to the gentility of 1930s' Hawai'i. Dishes include ono and ahi steak, lemon-ginger roasted chicken, and banana barbecue ribs. ◈ *Whalers Village, Kā'anapali • 667 6636 • Map B2 • $$$$*

3 CJ's Deli & Diner
Burgers, salads, sandwiches, and plate lunches, along with yummy baked goods made right on the premises. ◈ *At the Fairway Shops on Honoapi'ilani Highway, Kā'anapali • 5:30am–6pm daily • Map B2 • $*

4 Roy's Kahana Bar & Grill
Roy Yamaguchi's first Maui restaurant, serving up his trademark East-meets-West cuisine. Always bustling and busy, so book ahead. ◈ *At the Kahana Gateway Center • 669 6999 • Dinner only • Map C2 • $$$$$*

5 The Gazebo Restaurant
The oceanfront location could not be better at this breakfast and lunch restaurant. Fantastic banana pancakes! ◈ *5315 Lower Honoapi'ilani Rd. • 669 5621 • Map C2 • $*

6 Sea House Restaurant
Sample fresh sushi beside tranquil Nāpili Bay, or try the exquisite gingered pork loin. On Tuesday nights a hula show is presented by the children of the Nāpili Kai Foundation. ◈ *At Nāpili Kai Beach Resort • 669 1500 • Map C2 • $$$$*

7 Pizza Paradiso
A popular and award-winning spot for takeout or eat-in pizza, pasta, sandwiches, or desserts. Each slice of pizza weighs a pound. The tiramisu is wonderful. ◈ *3356 Lower Honoapi'ilani Parkway, Honokowai Marketplace • 667 2929 • Map C2 • $*

8 Sansei Seafood Restaurant & Sushi Bar
Amazing contemporary Japanese dishes, great service, and fun are perfectly blended here. ◈ *The Kapalua Resort, Honolua Village; 669 6286 • Map C1 • $$$ • Also Kīhei Town Center, 879 0004 (Map E4)*

9 Pineapple Grill
A delicious menu, dedication to local producers, excellent service, and stunning views make this a popular restaurant. ◈ *200 Kapalua Dr. • 669 9600 • Map C1 • $$$$*

10 Plantation House Restaurant at Kapalua
It's worth the drive to far Kapalua to sample Alex Stanislaw's singular Mediterranean-influenced cuisine. The signature Rich Forest Fish a must! ◈ *Plantation Course Clubhouse • 669 6299 • Map C1 • $$$$*

Note: Unless otherwise stated, all restaurants accept credit cards and serve vegetarian meals

Around Maui – West Maui

Left **Kanahā Beach** Center **Garden of the Bailey House Museum** Right **Sugar Museum**

Wailuku and Central Maui

NESTLED BETWEEN THE BEAUTIFUL PU'U KUKUI *(West Maui Mountains)* and the steep volcanic formation of Haleakalā to the east, Central Maui is not frequented by visitors nearly as much as the coastal resort areas. Yet it holds many cultural, historical, and natural attractions, as well as a wide variety of restaurants and a veritable bonanza of places for shopping. Wailuku, the county seat, lies at the base of 'Iao Valley and is full of funky antique shops and ethnic restaurants. The island's international airport and commercial harbor are in neighboring Kahului, along with shopping centers, a large park, and community services such as the hospital and police headquarters.

'Iao Valley

🔟 Sights

1 Maui Tropical Plantation

2 Ka'ahumanu Church

3 Bailey House Museum

4 'Iao Valley

5 Hawai'i Nature Center

6 Kepaniwai Park Gardens

7 Haleki'i Pihana Heiau

8 Alexander & Baldwin Sugar Museum

9 Kanahā Pond State Wildlife Sanctuary

10 Kanahā Beach Park

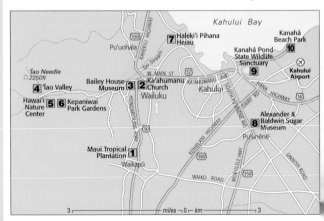

Maui Tropical Plantation

and artist Edward Bailey. Today, it houses the largest collection of pre-contact Hawaiian artifacts on public display on Maui, along with various missionary-era memorabilia, Bailey's original paintings, and fascinating historical photographs. *(See also pp14–15.)*

1 Maui Tropical Plantation

Located outside of Wailuku on Route 30, this attraction offers a glimpse into Maui's agricultural industry. There are displays and exhibits showing how 14 varieties of fruits and flowers are cultivated and processed; a mini tram tour through fields of sugar cane, pineapple, bananas, coffee, papaya, and macadamia plants; plus a store where the finished products can be bought. ◈ *Map N3* • *9am–5pm daily* • *Free; adm for tour*

2 Ka'ahumanu Church

A Wailuku landmark, the Ka'ahumanu Church was designed in New-England style by Edward Bailey, a Protestant missionary who lived in the house next door. The church was built in 1876 to honor Queen Ka'ahumanu, the powerful *ali'i* (monarch) whose influence was instrumental in establishing Christianity in the Hawaiian islands. Sunday services are conducted in the Hawaiian language. ◈ *Map N2*

3 Bailey House Museum

Bailey House is a missionary-era home built on an ancient royal Hawaiian site. The building was first used as a mission school and then as the home of missionary

4 'Iao Valley

The sacredness of this valley stretches far back into the pre-history of Hawai'i, but in more recent times it became known as the site of one of the bloodiest battles ever fought on Maui. Hundreds were killed in the 18th century when Kamehameha I waged war to unite the islands under his rule. The area is now a state park, with marked trails for hiking and the cool freshwater 'Iao Stream offering the respite of a cool dip on a hot day. *(See also pp10–11.)*

Ka'ahumanu Church

For hikes in Central Maui **See pp40–41**

5 Hawai'i Nature Center

A hands-on natural science center, filled with educational and entertaining indoor exhibits and outdoor experiences, all designed to increase understanding of Maui's unique environment. This innovative center, which fascinates children and adults alike, features interactive games and displays about the islands' plant and animal life, and teaches how to help protect the fragile ecosystems of Hawai'i. ✪ *Wailuku*
• *Map D3* • *244 6500* • *10am–4pm daily*
• *www.hawaiinaturecenter.org* • *Adm*

6 Kepaniwai Park Gardens

This peaceful park is a tribute to Maui's ethnic diversity. A leisurely stroll here reveals a replica of a traditional piece of architecture and a garden from each of the major contributors to Hawai'i's cultural mix: a Japanese tea house; a Chinese pagoda; a Portuguese villa; a Flipino abode; a New England frame house; and a traditional Hawaiian grass *hale* (house). Picnic areas with barbecue pits are set in the shade of trees by 'Īao Stream. *(See also pp10–11.)*

7 Haleki'i Pihana Heiau

One of Maui's most accessible archaeological sites, the remains of precontact Hawaiian

Kepaniwai Park Gardens

> ### Maui's Ethnic Mix
> Maui's Central Valley best points up Hawai'i's great ethnic diversity, probably because this region was home to the majority of plantation workers brought in from foreign shores. Today, the diversity shows up most in the dozens of wonderful ethnic restaurants and small businesses that dot Kahului and Wailuku.

structures here have both religious and historical importance. Haleki' Pihana was a chiefly compound, with thatched houses built atop a stone platform, and a *luakini* (human sacrificial temple). Signs explain the layout of the walls and terraces. The site is still used for traditional Hawaiian practices. ✪ *Map N1* • *Open access in daylight hours*

8 Alexander & Baldwin Sugar Museum

The sugar mill in Pu'unēnē is one of the last still operating in Hawai'i. Across the street from the mill stands the museum, housed in the plantation superintendent's residence of the early 20th century. Inside, the museum interestingly and informatively documents the history of Maui's sugar industry. Photographs, clothing, models, and artifacts illustrate what daily plantation life was like

Hawai'i Nature Center

for the owners and the immigrants who worked the fields and mills. ® Map Q1 • 871 8058 • www.sugarmuseum.com • Mon–Sat 9:30am–4:30pm • Adm

9 Kanahā Pond State Wildlife Sanctuary

Now a designated wildlife sanctuary, Kanahā was once a royal fishpond (see p98). Today it is a refuge for the rare Hawaiian stilt, or ae'o, as well as about 50 other bird species. The migratory ae'o is a slender wading bird that stands 16 inches tall and has a black back, white belly, and stick-like pink legs. The birds can often be seen feeding along the marshy edges of the pond near the Hāna Highway. ® Kahului • Map Q1 • Free

10 Kanahā Beach Park

Just off the road to the airport, the beach at Kanahā is narrow and the water usually choppy. But it's a great spot to windsurf and kite sail – or to watch more experienced practitioners. The park has large grassy areas, showers, restrooms, picnic tables, and barbecue pits. ® Map Q1

Kanahā Beach Park

Journey Through Time

Morning

🕐 Begin with an early morning visit to **Haleki'i Pihana Heiau**, perched on a bluff overlooking Maui's central valley. Take Route 340 from Kahului, make a left turn onto Kūhiū Place, and finally, turn onto Hea Place to reach the *Heiau* (temple). Maui's ancient chiefs would have surveyed their domain from this very spot.

Head back up Kahului's Ka'ahumanu Avenue all the way to the misty crags of **'Īao** (p71). Imagine the *ali'i* (royalty) enjoying this lush valley as you hike in the coolness of the tropical greenery and take a refreshing dip in the sparkling stream.

A ten-minute drive out of the valley to Wailuku will bring you to **Bailey House Museum** (p71) for a look at precontact life on Maui. Bailey's own paintings also provide an interesting glimpse into how the island looked when the Protestant missionaries arrived in the 1820s.

Afternoon

Grab a quick, local-style lunch at Sam Sato's or Wei Wei Noodles & Barbecue, both in the nearby Wailuku Millyard.

Next, you come to the island's plantation era, vividly displayed at the **Alexander & Baldwin Sugar Museum**. And to bring you back up to date, end your day by picking up some *pūpū* (snacks) at one of the many markets in Kahului – Safeway, Ah Fook's, Foodland – then head to **Kanahā Beach Park** for a sunset picnic.

Price Categories

Price categories include a three-course meal for one, a glass of house wine, and all unavoidable extra charges including tax.	**$** under $20
	$$ $20–$30
	$$$ $30–$45
	$$$$ $45–$60
	$$$$$ over $60

Left **Ruby's Diner** Right **Marco's Grill & Deli**

Places to Eat and Nightlife

1 Thailand Cuisine
Tucked into the Maui Mall, the menu offers all the Thai favorites; the Pad Thai is especially good. ◈ *70 Ka'ahumanu Ave., Kahului • Map P2 • 873 0225 • $$*

2 Asian Star
Simply delectable Vietnamese food at great prices. Try the tangerine beef or sesame chicken. ◈ *1764 Wili Pa Loop, off Mill St. • Map N1 • 244 1833 • $$*

3 Tokyo Tei
You won't find fresher sashimi, more luscious salmon teriyaki, friendlier service, or better value anywhere on Maui than at this family owned Wailuku institution. ◈ *1063 East Lower Main St. • Map N/P1 • 242 9630 • $$*

4 A.K.'s Café
Chef Elaine Rothermel's delightful place offers delicious local-style food, a modern bar, contemporary Hawaiian entertainment, and a welcoming atmosphere. ◈ *1237 Lower Main St., Wailuku • Map N2 • 244 8774 • $$*

5 Stillwell's Bakery & Café
Sometimes, you just want a fresh, crisp salad or a thick, hearty sandwich – so head for this place on the border between Wailuku and Kahului. Operated by top pastry chef, Roy Stillwell and his wife, it would be a crime to bypass dessert here. ◈ *Breakfast pastries and lunch • 1740 Ka'ahumanu Ave. • Map P2 • 243 2243 • $*

6 Maui Arts & Cultural Center
This $50-million complex houses several theaters and an art gallery. Everyone from Tony Bennett to the Brothers Cazimero perform here; there's something going on every day. ◈ *One Cameron Way, off Kahului Beach Rd. • Map P1 • 242 2787, 242 7469*

7 A Saigon Café
Vietnamese "burritos," whole steamed fish, fried lobster, rice bowl, and other specialties have all found their way into the hearts – and bellies – of locals. Unusually for Maui, the café stays open right through from lunch to dinner. ◈ *1792 Main St. • Map N2 • 243 9560 • $$*

8 Ruby's Diner
A cool, sleek, 1950s style burger joint (part of a regional chain), which serves up huge breakfast platters, juicy burgers, crisp fries, shakes, and giant salads. ◈ *Queen Ka'ahumanu Center, Ka'ahumanu Ave., Kahului • Map P2 • 248 7829 • $*

9 Marco's Grill & Deli
A favorite for Italian sandwiches, pasta, veal, chicken, and fish dishes, plus calorie-packed desserts. ◈ *444 Hāna Highway • Map Q2 • 877 4446 • $$$*

10 Café Marc Aurel
This popular hangout offers lunch, a wine and cheese bar, and an art gallery. ◈ *28 N. Market St., Wailuku • Map N1 • 244 0852 • $$*

Note: *Unless otherwise stated, all restaurants accept credit cards and serve vegetarian meals*

Left **Queen Ka'ahumanu Center** Center **Maui Marketplace** Right **Borders Books, Music & Café**

 # Shopping Places

1 Bailey House Gift Shop
A large selection of quality products made in Hawai'i are available in this small shop, including *lua hala* hats and hand-sewn feather hatbands, jams and jellies, music CDs, and cookbooks. 🛇 *2375-A Main St. • 244 3326 • Map N1*

2 Bird of Paradise Unique Antiques
A treasure trove of 1930s to '50s glassware, tableware, furniture, and plenty of Hawaiiana. 🛇 *56 N. Market St. • 242 7699 • Map N1*

3 Maui Thing
Created by a local designer and produced on Maui, the tees, tanks, dresses, and accessories in this store are designed to inspire clean living. 🛇 *7 N. Market St. • 249 0215 • Map N1*

4 Queen Ka'ahumanu Center
Maui's largest shopping center, this two-level mall is where you'll find national chains like Macy's, Sears, and Ben Franklin, alongside quintessentially local stores like Camelia Seed Shop (local snacks). 🛇 *275 Ka'ahumanu Ave. • Map P2*

5 Maui Mall
Kahului's other shopping center, anchored by Longs Drug Store and Star Market. Cost Less Imports is fun, and Kahului Florist is a good place for *lei* (garlands). 🛇 *70 Ka'ahumanu Ave. • Map P2*

6 Longs Drug Stores
A pharmacy, on-site photo processing, local foodstuffs, toiletries, stationery items, magazines, and even rubber slippers: it's all at Longs. 🛇 *Maui Mall, Kahului; Map P2 • Also at Longs Center (Kīhei), and Lahaina Cannery Mall*

7 Safeway
The supermarket's deli is fabulous, and the on-site bakery turns out the best artisan breads on the Island. 🛇 *Kamehameha Ave.; Map P2 • Also at Kīhei and Lahaina*

8 Maui Swap Meet
Locals get here early for the best selection of fresh flowers and produce. There are also lots of T-shirts, inexpensive gift items, and the stuff folks have cleaned out of their garages. 🛇 *Maui Community College Campus • Sat early morning to noon • Map P/Q2*

9 Maui Marketplace
Sports Authority, Lowe's Home Improvement Center, Old Navy, and Office Max have outlets here. The locally owned Hawai'i Liquor Superstore has an outstanding selection of wines. 🛇 *Dairy Road • Map Q2*

10 Borders Books, Music & Café
The vast stock includes a full selection of Hawaiian music and books, while the café serves good coffee, breakfast items, and light lunches. 🛇 *Maui Marketplace, Dairy Road • 877 6160 • Map Q2*

Around Maui – Wailuku and Central Maui

Left **Humpback Whales National Marine Center** Center **Keālia Pond** Right **Waterfront Restaurant**

South Maui

*S*UNNY SOUTH MAUI, *on the island's leeward coast, is fringed by white sand beaches hugging the shimmering blue Pacific, with Lāna'i, Molokini, and Kaho'olawe rising up from the ocean within full view. Just "mauka" (toward the mountain) of the first stretch of beaches is the well-populated area of Kīhei, crowded with an overwhelming profusion of condominium complexes, small shopping malls, and oft times tedious traffic. Once you hit the beach, however, you'll soon relax into tropical mode. Traveling south takes you to the manicured resort area of Wailea and the much less developed Mākena district.*

Whale-watching beach near Kīhei

🔟 Sights

1. Maui Ocean Center
2. Māʻalaea Small Boat Harbor
3. Keālia Pond National Wildlife Refuge
4. Hawaiian Island Humpback Whales National Marine Sanctuary
5. Mākena
6. Keawalaʻi Congregational Church
7. Puʻu Ōlaʻi
8. ʻĀhihi-Kinaʻu Natural Area Reserve
9. La Pérouse Bay
10. Hoapili Trail

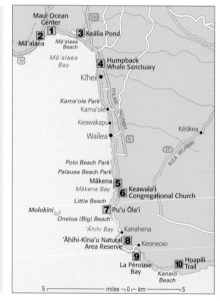

Previous pages **Surfing the big waves**

1 Maui Ocean Center

An up-close experience of Pacific marine life, such as sea turtles, rays, and whales, for those who don't want to get wet. Visitors can view sharks while walking through a 50-ft-long clear acrylic tunnel, and they are invited to touch harmless marine animals such as sea stars and sea cucumbers at the Discovery Pool. ◈ *Map D4* • *9am–5pm daily* • *www.mauioceancenter.com* • *Adm*

Maui Ocean Center

2 Māʻalaea Small Boat Harbor

A popular surfing spot, Māʻalaea Harbor marks the beginning of a three-mile stretch of beaches that reaches to North Kīhei. Boat charters depart from here for fishing trips and snorkeling excursions to Molokini. During the winter, Maui's most famous visitors, the humpback whales, breed in the warm waters of the bay, and whale-watching tours set off from the harbor several times a day. ◈ *Map D4*

3 Keālia Pond National Wildlife Refuge

One of the few natural wetlands remaining in the Hawaiian islands, these 691 acres are often referred to locally – and not particularly correctly – as the "mud flats." Located along the coast just north of Kīhei, the refuge shelters endangered birds such as Hawaiian stilts *(aeʻo)* and Hawaiian coots *(ʻalae keʻokeʻo)* and protects the coastal sand dunes, which provide nesting habitat for endangered hawksbill sea turtles. Pink-legged stilts are easily seen from the road. ◈ *Map E4* • *7:30am–4pm Mon–Fri* • *Closed public hols*

4 Hawaiian Island Humpback Whales National Marine Sanctuary

In its entirety, the sanctuary almost completely encompasses the ocean surrounding the Hawaiian islands. But its administrative center sits on the water's edge at Kīhei, with a large viewing scope mounted on its deck for winter visitors to watch the humpback whales frolic offshore. In the adjoining Education Center, colorful displays depict the scientific and cultural significance of whales and other marine animals that share Hawaiʻi's marine ecosystem. ◈ *Kīhei* • *Map E4* • *Education Center: Mon–Fri 10am–3pm; free* • *www.hawaiihumpbackwhale.noaa.gov*

Māʻalaea Small Boat Harbor

Mākena Beach

Mākena

5 Fairly far from the madding crowds, the Mākena Resort has only one hotel – The Maui Prince – and two golf courses, both designed by Robert Trent Jones, Jr. The natural highlight of the Mākena area is Oneloa (Big Beach), a 3,000-ft long dazzling white sand beach. In days long gone, Mākena was a busy port. *Paniolo* (Portuguese cowboys) drove their cattle down the slopes of Haleakalā to be prodded into the surf at Mākena Landing, then lashed to shore boats and taken to waiting barges for shipment to market in Honolulu. *(See pp16–17.)*

Keawala'i Congregational Church

6 This lovely little church, built in 1832, sits in a shady palm grove at the edge of the sea. Prayers and hymns are offered in the

'Āhihi-Kina'u National Area Reserve

Humpback Migration

From their summer home in distant Alaska, majestic humpback whales migrate to Maui's warm waters every winter to give birth and nurture their young. An endangered species, humpbacks are known for their playful acrobatics and haunting songs – whistles, groans, and screeches – that comprise their unique language.

Hawaiian language during services held each Sunday morning. In typical local style, visitors are asked to remove their shoes before entering. Many hundreds of Mauians, as well as a fair few visitors, have been married at Keawala'i. Ⓢ *Map E5*

Pu'u Ōla'i

7 This 360-ft tall, red-hued cinder cone was formed by Haleakalā's last eruption in the late 1700s. It separates Oneloa from "Little Beach," which, partly because of its sheltered location, is a popular clothing-optional beach. However, you should be aware that nudity on public beaches is technically illegal in Hawai'i. Ⓢ *Map E6*

8 'Āhihi-Kina'u Natural Area Reserve

Walking trails through the dramatic lava fields of this reserve lead to natural pools and archaeological sites. And, in the underwater sections, terrific snorkeling and scuba diving can be found. This is a reserve, however, and visitors are reminded that damaging or removing anything of the natural habitat is strictly illegal. Map E–F6

9 La Pérouse Bay

French explorer La Pérouse sailed into this bay in 1786, noting that the people "hastened alongside in their canoes, bringing as articles of commerce, hogs, potatoes, bananas, taro with cloth and some other curiosities." Named after this first westerner to land on Maui's shores, the bay is a great snorkeling and diving spot. (See also pp16 & 32.) Map E6

10 Hoapili Trail

This 7-mile hike over rugged and barren terrain moves uphill from the ocean then meanders back toward the coastline. Along the seaside road, stone walls and raised platforms of *heiau* (temples) and *hale* (houses) are still visible. The hike requires sturdy shoes. (See also pp17 & 40.) Map F6

La Pérouse Bay

Fun in the Sun

Morning

🕐 Slather on the sunscreen, grab a mask, snorkel, and fins, and put on your hat for a morning of Maui's fabled sun, sand, and sea. The trade winds here normally pick up between 11am and 1pm, so early morning is the time to claim your spot at any one of the sparkling white beaches that line the Kīhei/Wailea coast. **Kama'ole I, II, or III, Keawakapu,** and **Wailea** *(see pp42–3)* are all perfect for swimming, snorkeling, body boarding, or just plain sunning. Farther south, Big Beach at **Mākena** is entirely idyllic, and **La Pérouse Bay** shelters fabulous snorkeling and kayaking spots.

It's best to be out of the sun well before noon, and that's a good time to head to **Alexander's Fish & Chips**, Kīhei Caffe, or one of the many food stops that dot South Kīhei Road.

Afternoon

The **Hawaiian Island Humpback Whales National Marine Sanctuary** provides a good after-lunch activity. You'll learn about the wonders of Hawai'i's marine life, most notably the gentle giants that winter in these waters. Binoculars and viewing stands are available at no charge. Right in front of the sanctuary's office deck, and easily seen with the naked eye, are the remains of an ancient fish pond (currently being restored).

There's a small park adjacent to the sanctuary's buildings where you can enjoy an afternoon snack or a thirst-quenching drink at a shady table.

Left **Azeka's Place** Right **Kukui Mall**

Shopping

1 Azeka Makai & Mauka
The former houses the post office, souvenir shops, fast food joints, a florist, a bakery, and several professional services such as a dentist and travel agency. Across the road, Azeka Mauka offers local banks, more souvenirs, and Stella Blues *(see opposite)*. ⊗ *South Kīhei Rd.* • *Map E4*

2 Pi'ilani Village Center
Mainlanders will feel right at home amid Blockbusters, Starbucks, Jamba Juice, and Hawai'i's largest Safeway. For local flavor, Roy's Kīhei is a good choice, as is Hilo Hattie *(see below)*. ⊗ *225 Pi'ikea Ave., Kīhei* • *Map E4*

3 Hilo Hattie
Once regarded as nothing more than a tacky tourist dive, Hilo Hattie has branched outward and upward, and now even locals browse the racks of better quality aloha wear. ⊗ *Pi'ilani Village Center, Kīhei* • *Map E4* • *Also in Lahaina and Kā'anapali*

4 Kukui Mall
This is the home of K'ihei's only movie theaters. You can snack at one of the many eateries offering pizzas, sandwiches, and Thai food. ⊗ *1819 S. Kīhei Rd., Kīhei* • *Map E4*

5 Kīhei Kalama Village Marketplace
A group of open-air stalls, where you can search out some "crafted-in-Hawai'i" items. ⊗ *Opposite Kalama Beach Park, Kīhei* • *Map E4*

6 Clementine's
A long-time Maui resident, Clementine magically crams a treasure trove of unique clothing, jewelry, accessories, and more into a joyous cupboard of a room! ⊗ *1941D South Kīhei Rd.* • *Map E4*

7 Rainbow Mall & Kama'ole Shopping Center
The former offers souvenirs and resort wear, and has a great little kiosk called Maui Espresso. The latter is home to 24-hour eatery Denny's, postal services, and Whalers General Store, for everything from toiletries to souvenirs. ⊗ *2439 South Kīhei Rd.* • *Map E4*

8 The Shops at Wailea
Maui's most upscale shopping complex features international names like Tiffany & Co., Gucci, and Banana Republic alongside local retailers, such as Honolua Surf Co. for casual wear and Martin & MacArthur for stunning wood furniture. ⊗ *Wailea* • *Map E5*

9 Cy Maui
Beautiful, unique, hand-painted and silk clothing, much of it locally made. ⊗ *The Shops at Wailea* • *Map E5*

10 Blue Ginger
For those who enjoy more subtle versions of Hawaiian prints, Blue Ginger offers some great designs. It is especially good for baby and children's clothes. ⊗ *The Shops at Wailea* • *Map E5* • *Also at Whalers Village & Queen Ka'ahumanu Center*

Share your travel recommendations on traveldk.com

Price Categories

Price categories include a three-course meal for one, a glass of house wine, and all unavoidable extra charges including tax.

$	under $20
$$	$20–$30
$$$	$30–$45
$$$$	$45–$60
$$$$$	over $60

Alexander's Fish & Chips

🔟 Places to Eat & Nightlife

1 Waterfront Restaurant
The name says it all. Literally at the ocean's edge, fresh fish prepared in several different ways each night is why the Waterfront has such staying power. ◎ 50 Hau'oli St., Mā'alaea • Map D4 • 244 9028 • Dinner only • $$$$$

2 Stella Blues
Now in bigger and better digs at Azeka Mauka, the very popular Stella Blues takes its name from a song by California's Grateful Dead. Try the tofu scramble for breakfast – one of many vegetarian selections. ◎ Azeka Mauka, South Kīhei Rd. • Map E4 • 874 3779 • $$

3 Shaka Sandwich & Pizza
Nostalgic East Coasters will be sated at this unassuming little restaurant, which serves the best pizza this side of Brooklyn and the best Philly cheesesteaks this side of, well, Philadelphia. ◎ 1770 South Kīhei Rd., • Map E4 • 874 0331 • $

4 Alexander's Fish & Chips
Fresh fish, shrimp, chicken, and potatoes are fried in canola oil (or broiled if you prefer). Perfect for a picnic lunch on one of Kīhei's beaches. ◎ 1913 South Kīhei Rd. • Map E4 • 874 0788 • $

5 Joe's Bar & Grill
Fresh fish, steak, and ribs are served at this lovely open-air restaurant. Great desserts and an excellent wine list. ◎ Wailea Tennis Center • Map E5 • 875 7767 • Dinner only • $$$$

6 Sarento's on the Beach
You can't get closer to the beach than Sarento's. Corporate Chef George Gomes oversees the menu of contemporary Italian favorites, rustled up with island flair. ◎ 2980 South Kīhei Rd. • Map E4 • 875 7555 • Dinner only • $$$$$

7 Tommy Bahama's Tropical Café
Next to its namesake clothing store, this casual restaurant serves well-prepared Pacific Rim salads, appetizers, and entrees. ◎ Map E5 • The Shops at Wailea • 879 9983 • $$

8 Lulu's
Enjoy good food, exotic drinks, karaoke, salsa dancing, and live music – all with an ocean view – at this fun venue. ◎ 1945 South Kīhei Rd. • Map E4 • 879 9944 • $$

9 Spago
Fresh fish, creatively prepared desserts, stunning presentations, and city-style service are the hallmarks of Wolfgang Puck's aquatically styled restaurant. ◎ Four Seasons Resort, Wailea • Map E5 • 874 8000 • Dinner only • $$$$$

10 Sea Watch Restaurant
Exceptional ocean and mountain views are matched by the menu created by Maui celebrity chef Bev Gannon. The restaurant is located in the grounds of the Gold & Emerald Golf Course (see p47). ◎ 100 Wailea Golf Club Dr. • Map E5 • 875 8080 • $$$$$

Note: Unless otherwise stated, all restaurants accept credit cards and serve vegetarian meals

Left **Polli's restaurant, Makawao** Right **Hui No'eau Visual Arts Center**

North Shore and Upcountry

THE NORTH SHORE OF MAUI *is sculpted by the winds and waves, its coastline traced by the winding road to Hāna. This is the lush tropical side of the island with verdant forests fed by sparkling waterfalls. Higher in elevation, on Haleakalā's west-facing slope, is the area referred to locally as Upcountry. This broad expanse of rolling pastures and fertile farmlands is famous for its* paniolo (cowboy) *tradition and fabulous produce.*

Left **Haleakalā National Park** Right **'Ulupalakua Ranch, Statue**

🗺 Sights

1. Pā'ia Town
2. Ho'okipa
3. Makawao Union and Holy Rosary Churches
4. Hui No'eau Visual Arts Center
5. Makawao Town
6. Holy Ghost Church
7. Haleakalā National Park
8. Dr. Sun Yat-sen Memorial Park
9. Tedeschi Winery
10. 'Ulupalakua Ranch

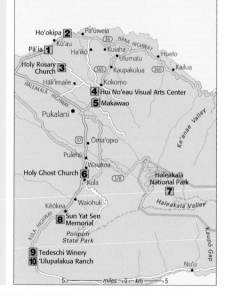

Pā'ia Town

1 Pā'ia Town

Once a large and busy sugar plantation town, the mill and residential camps that surrounded it are gone. Now Pā'ia, which straddles Hāna Highway, bustles with boutiques, shops, a health food store, an artisans' cooperative, and casual eateries. Technically, the road to Hāna really begins here, and it's wise to pick up a picnic and fill the car before embarking on the long and winding road. 🛇 Map G2

2 Ho'okipa

Waves come crashing in at heights of up to 15 ft (4.5 m) onto Ho'okipa Beach, ensuring its renown as a playground for experienced surfers and windsurfers. But it is also a glorious spot for the less experienced to watch the skills of the dedicated boarders, especially during the international championship competitions held here. The best vantage for a view of the ocean is from high up at the overlook above the beach. 🛇 Map G2

3 Makawao Union and Holy Rosary Churches

Charming Makawao Union Church was built in stone by Hawai'i's most famous modern architect, C. W. Dickey, as a chapel for the Baldwins, a missionary, industrialist, and generously philanthropic family. Across the road stands the Holy Rosary Church and, outside it, a statue of the beatified Father Damien *(see p27)*. 🛇 Baldwin Avenue, between Pā'ia and Makawao • Map G3

4 Hui No'eau Visual Arts Center

Founded in 1936 by Ethel Baldwin, wife of Maui's political and business leader Harry Baldwin, as a "club of skills" to exercise her creative talents, Hui No'eau showcases the work of local artists. The center resides in Kaluanui, the home designed by C. W. Dickey for the Baldwins in 1917. The spacious mansion is a splendid example of Dickey's style. 🛇 Map G3 • 10am–4pm Mon–Sat • www.huinoeau.com • Donation

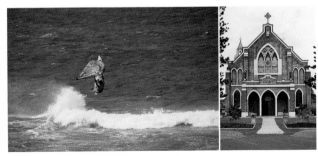
Left **Windsurfer at Ho'okipa** Right **Holy Rosary Church**

Makawao Town

Makawao Town

5 Reminiscent of a western movie set, Makawao's big day comes on the 4th of July, when cowboys, cowgirls, and their horses, along with a bevy of unusual floats, parade through town as a prelude to the annual rodeo. The rest of the year, the adventure lies in the boutiques, art galleries, and New Age shops that crowd the sidewalks. Not to be missed is Komoda's, a family-owned bakery that's been delighting customers with yummy cream puffs for 60 years. ✎ *Map G3*

Holy Ghost Church

6 Affectionately referred to as the "wedding cake" church, this octagonal white building glistens in the sun above Lower Kula Highway. It was built in 1895 by Portuguese immigrants, who, having fulfilled their contracts with the sugar plantations, settled Upcountry as farmers and ranchers. Austrian master woodcarver Ferdinand Stuflesser created the ornate altar and stations of the cross, both extremely fine examples of 19th-century ecclesiastical art. Today, Holy Ghost's "bread ladies" bake equally fine examples of Portuguese sweet bread. ✎ *Map F4*

Haleakalā National Park

7 Atop Haleakalā, the 10,023-ft mountain that IS East Maui, lies the massive basin of a dormant volcano. The summit is an awesome landscape of cinder cones, rare plants and animals, amazing vistas, and trails. *(See pp20–21.)*

The Paniolo Tradition

British explorer Captain George Vancouver brought cattle to Hawai'i in 1793 and soon the animals were running amok in island forests. In 1832, Mexican *vacqueros* (ranchers) arrived to teach Hawaiians how to deal with the roaming cattle. That was the beginning of Hawai'i's cowboy, or *paniolo*, tradition (*paniolo* being the Hawaiian corruption of *español*, a reference to the Spanish spoken by the Mexican *vacqueros*).

Haleakalā National Park

Sign up for DK's email newsletter on traveldk.com

Tedeschi Winery

8 Dr. Sun Yat-sen Memorial Park

A statue of the revolutionary Dr. Sun Yat-sen, the first president of the Republic of China, stands in this small park in Keokea. His brother, Sun Mei, was one of the many Chinese immigrants who settled in this area, and the doctor hid his family here with him during the Chinese Revolution of 1911. The park occupies around 6,000 acres of land that once belonged to his brother. ◈ *Map G4*

9 Tedeschi Winery

Free daily tours and tastings are held at Tedeschi, Maui's only winery. Established in 1974, Tedeschi produces sparkling, red, and blush wines, and its most famous product, Maui Blanc, a sweet pineapple wine. ◈ *Map F5*
• *9am–5pm daily* • *Free tours at 10:30am, 1:30pm & 3pm* • *www.mauiwine.com*

10 'Ulupalakua Ranch

Ship captain James Makee established the ranch in 1856 and built a house for his large family, cisterns to capture water, a sugar mill to generate income, and a cottage for his frequent guest, King Kalākaua. Today, the house is gone, the cisterns are filled in, the sugar mill lies in ruins, and the restored King's Cottage is Tedeschi Winery's tasting room. 'Ulupalakua continues, however, as a working ranch, and many of Maui's *paniolo* (cowboys) ride its 20,000-acre range. ◈ *Map F5*

A Day in the Hills

Morning

Spend some time away from the sand and surf by heading up the Haleakalā Highway (Route 37) to the coolness of Upcountry Maui. At 'Ulupalakua Ranch you'll find the **Tedeschi Winery**. Tours of the winery are free, and you can taste the full range of products in the restored cottage of King David Kalākaua.

Retrace your path back along Route 37 to visit Makawao, once a cowboy town and now a shopper's haven. There are tony boutiques and art galleries housed in western-style buildings. Pick up some lunch at Rodeo General Store's deli or pastries at Komoda's Bakery, both on Baldwin Ave., the town's "main drag."

Afternoon

Continue down Baldwin Avenue to the **Hui No'eau Visual Arts Center**. Inside and outside, works by local artists are created, displayed, and sold. Traveling right to the end of Baldwin Avenue will take you to Pā'ia for great people watching – and more shopping. Once a plantation town, then a hippie haven, and now a windsurfing mecca, Pā'ia offers an adventure in browsing for unique clothing at **Jagger's** (see p88), work by local artists at Maui Hands, and antiques at **Pā'ia Trading Company** (p88).

For a late afternoon spectacle, the waters off Ho'okipa Beach are filled with the colorful sails of windsurfers and kite boarders. Finally, end your day with a fresh fish dinner at **Mama's Fish House** (p89).

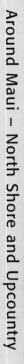

Around Maui – North Shore and Upcountry

For more about 'Ulupalakua Ranch, see pp18–19

Left **Maui Crafts Guild** Right **Gecko Trading Company**

TOP 10 Shopping

1 Maui Crafts Guild
If you're looking for artistic souvenirs or gifts, this collective of Maui artisans is the place for you. Almost every medium is represented. ⬡ *69 Hāna Highway, Pā'ia • Map G2 • www.mauicraftsguild.com*

2 Pā'ia Trading Company
Take your time perusing the collectibles here – glass bottles, aloha shirts, jewelry, and more. You may just find an affordable treasure. ⬡ *106 Hāna Highway, Pā'ia • Map G2*

3 Maui Girl & Co.
Young women – and others lucky enough to be able to squeeze into "smallish" sizes – will especially enjoy shopping here for swimsuits – mostly fabulous bikinis – and casual clothing. ⬡ *12 Baldwin Ave., Pā'ia • Map G2*

4 Jaggers
Casual aloha wear hangs side by side with dressier frocks for women and aloha shirts for men, forming the stock in trade of this well-known Pā'ia shop. ⬡ *100 Hāna Highway, Pā'ia • Map G2*

5 Viewpoints Gallery
This artists' collective is worth a look even if you're not in the market for art. Evening receptions for exhibition openings are held often, and these social gatherings provide a great opportunity to mix with Maui's locals. ⬡ *3620 Baldwin Ave., Makawao • Map G3*

6 Hot Island Glass
You can watch artisans demonstrate the skill of glass blowing in this combined studio and shop. And then, of course, you can buy the wares – from paperweights to exquisite vases. ⬡ *3620 Baldwin Ave., Makawao • Map G3*

7 Gecko Trading Company
A charming and diverse merchandise mix is what Gecko is all about. You'll find casual clothing, fashionable T-shirts, handbags, jewelry, small home decor items, and gifts. ⬡ *3621 Baldwin Ave., Makawao • Map G3*

8 Rodeo General Store
Known for its delicious deli foods and excellent wine selection, Rodeo also administers to regular grocery needs too. And yup, every now and again a cowboy rides up on horseback. ⬡ *3661 Baldwin Ave., Makawao • Map G3*

9 Collections
Lovely and comfortable clothing, accessories, jewelry, bath items, housewares, and one of the best selections of greeting cards on the island. ⬡ *3677 Baldwin Avenue, Makawao • Map G3*

10 Altitude
This tiny boutique is well stocked with distinctive women's apparel and accessories, including unusual, yet interesting, designer jewelry and cashmere pashminas. ⬡ *3660 Baldwin Avenue, Makawao • Map G3*

Price Categories

Price categories include a three-course meal for one, a glass of house wine, and all unavoidable extra charges including tax.

$	under $20
$$	$20–$30
$$$	$30–$45
$$$$	$45–$60
$$$$$	over $60

Left **Charley's** Right **Mama's Fish House**

Places to Eat

1 Mama's Fish House

Mama's heart-stirring beachside setting makes for a fine dining experience. The *mahi mahi* steamed in traditional *lu'au* leaves is a must-try. ✪ *79 Poho Pl., Kū'au • Map G2 • 579 8488 • $$$$$*

2 Moana Café

Off the beaten path, but well worth a detour for the fresh, unfussy, well-prepared food. The baked goods and fish specials are always good bets here. ✪ *71 Baldwin Ave., Pā'ia • Map G2 • 579 9999 • $$*

3 Charley's

Gigantic, home-style breakfasts, pizza, and burgers, along with the possible company of Willie Nelson or Kris Kristofferson, both of whom have been known to drop in. ✪ *142 Hāna Highway, Pā'ia • Map G2 • 579 9453 • $$*

4 Pa'uwela Café

It's not an easy place to find, but specialties like the kālua turkey sandwich and baker Becky Speere's delightful pastries make it more than worth the trouble. ✪ *375 W. Kuiaha Rd., Ha'ikū • Map G2 • 575 9242 • $*

5 Hana Hou Café

One of Maui's few places to serve traditional Hawaiian foods like *kālua* pork, *poi*, and *laulau*. There's a good mix of other ethnic dishes, like pasta and sashimi, too. ✪ *810 Ha'ikū Rd., Ha'ikū • Map G2 • 575 2661 • $$*

6 Hāli'imaile General Store

Smack in the middle of a pineapple plantation 1,200 ft up Haleakalā, Beverly Gannon's superb Hawai'i regional cooking with international influences ensures that this is a trek well worth making. ✪ *900 Hāli'imaile Rd., Hāli'imaile • Map G3 • 572 2666 • $$$$$*

7 Flatbread

Drop in for all-natural pizzas topped with local ingredients and baked in a wood-fired oven, plus farm-fresh salads. ✪ *89 Hāna Highway, Pā'ia • Map G2 • 579 8989 • $*

8 Komoda's Bakery

Everyone but everyone comes here for the cream puffs. But come early – nearly everything sells out before lunchtime. ✪ *3674 Baldwin Ave., Makawao • Map G3 • $*

9 Polli's

All things Mexican – including big, frothy margaritas – are served at this down-home favorite. Be sure to try the cashew garlic salad dressing and tasty salsa. ✪ *1202 Makawao Ave., Makawao • Map G3 • 572 7808 • $$*

10 Casanova Italian Restaurant & Deli

The deli serves great cappuccino, delicious breakfasts, and light lunches. And the adjacent restaurant serves delectable pizzas from a wood-fired oven, creative Italian fare, and fresh fish nightly. ✪ *1188 Makawao Ave., Makawao • Map G3 • 572 0220 • $$$$*

 Note: *Unless otherwise stated, all restaurants accept credit cards and serve vegetarian meals*

Left **Kau'iki Hill** Center **Roadside fruit stand** Right **Hāna Cultural Center**

East Maui

EAST MAUI IS THE STUFF OF TRAVEL POSTERS – *lush and tropical with cascading waterfalls, refreshing pools tucked into mountainside crevices, luxuriant foliage, and the most brilliant flowers. Almost equal to what it possesses, however, is what it does not – no resort developments, no modern housing complexes, no fast food joints, and no need to hurry. The only town, Hāna, is reached by way of a serpentine road (an attraction in itself), with panoramic ocean views and many wayside parks.*

Left **Huialoha Church** Right **Cattle ranch**

🔟 Sights

1. The Road to Hāna
2. Garden of Eden Arboretum
3. Wailua
4. Pi'ilanihale Heiau
5. Wai'anapanapa State Park
6. Hanā Cultural Center
7. Kau'iki Hill
8. Waimoku Falls
9. Palapala Ho'omau Church
10. Huialoha Church

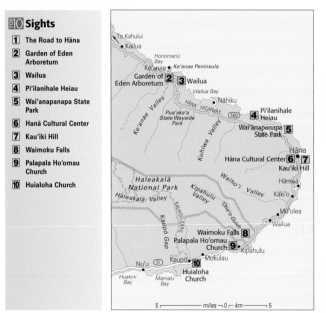

Previous pages **Pu'u 'Ula'ula summit, Haleakalā**

Road to Hāna

1 The Road to Hāna

Famed as one of the world's most scenic drives, Hāna Highway follows the coastline from Kahului, winding through rain forests dotted with the bright orange blossoms of African tulip trees and huge bamboo thickets waving in the breeze. The route passes waterfalls tumbling into pools and wends among trees laden with banana, mango, and mountain apple. Keep your windows open to experience the heady fragrances. *(See pp22–3.)*

2 Garden of Eden Arboretum

The Garden of Eden is filled with native and indigenous species as well as exotic plants, trees, and birds from the South Pacific and tropical rain forests of the world. Botanical labels identify more than 500 plants, including the most extensive collection of Ti plants in Hawai'i. Visitors can picnic, stroll, hike, or just breathe in the flowers' aromas in these 26 acres of gardens and arboretum. ◎ *10600 Hāna Highway* • *Map J3* • *8am–3pm* • *Adm*

3 Wailua

Marked out by its *lo'i kalo* (taro patches), the village of Wailua is just over halfway along the road to Hāna. Native Hawaiians raise and tend the precious plants in the traditional way of their ancestors. At mile marker 18, you can turn left onto Wailua Road, go past St. Gabriel's Church and the Miracle of Fatima Shrine, and reach an easily accessible and highly refreshing waterfall. ◎ *Map J3*

4 Pi'ilanihale Heiau

Thanks to an extensive restoration, many stone walls and platforms of this *heiau* (temple) are complete and provide a fascinating look at one of the largest of these traditional religious sites in Hawai'i. The platforms and huge stone walls, some more than 50 ft high, are surrounded by Kahanu Gardens. The gardens contain culturally important plants including the world's largest collection of breadfruit trees (120 varieties), one of Hawai'i's last undisturbed native *hala* (pandanus) forests, and varieties of coconut, banana, vanilla, and *'awa* (kava). ◎ *Map K4* • *Gardens: Mon–Fri 10am–2pm (but times do vary)* • *248 8912* • *Adm*

Garden of Eden Arboretum

Wai'anapanapa State Park

the cone. A cave at its base was the birthplace of Queen Ka'ahumanu *(see p23)*. Ⓢ *Map L4*

Wai'ānapanapa State Park
The natural features of this park include freshwater spring-fed caves, a magnificent black sand beach, *heiau* (temples), blowholes, the King's Trail *(see p41)*, and a fascinating natural stone arch traversing towering peaks of lava. Ⓢ *Map L4*

Hāna Cultural Center
The Hāna Cultural Center and its museum has displays of artifacts from the district, including stone implements, kapa cloth, quilts, and an extensive shell collection. *(See also p23.)*

Kau'iki Hill
This large cinder cone, which in ancient Hawai'i provided fortification against invaders, today guards Hāna Bay. The hill and its beach are deep red in color due to the iron-rich lava that forms

Waimoku Falls
One of Maui's tallest, Waimoku Falls cascades more than 400 ft into 'Ohe'o Gulch in the Kīpahulu District of Haleakalā National Park. Hikers can reach the falls by taking the Waimoku Falls Trail *(see p25)*. Ⓢ *Map K5*

Palapala Ho'omau Church
The Palapala Ho'omau Church stands eight miles past Hāna town on the *makai* (ocean) side of the road. Famed American aviator Charles Lindbergh helped repair the church, following its decline into a state of dilapidation. Lindbergh also chose the church for his final resting place. He designed his own grave, which can be seen behind the church marked with river stones. Ⓢ *Map K5*

Huialoha Church
Standing next to Mokulau Beach on a desolate and beautiful stretch of coast, Huialoha Church was saved from ruin by members of the communities of Hāna, Kīpahulu, and Kaupō. It was built in 1859 in a style reminiscent of New England churches, with white walls and a prim steeple. Ⓢ *Kaupō • Map K6*

Kalo, Corm, and Poi
Kalo (taro) is the most important food crop to native Hawaiians. Grown in *lo'i* (patches), the plant has big, beautiful, heart-shaped leaves and grows about one foot tall, rising from an underground – or underwater – stem called the corm. The corm is pounded into *poi*, the nutrient-packed staple starch of the Hawaiians.

Waimoku Falls

For an East Maui itinerary, see The Road to Hāna feature, pp22–3

Left **Hāna Coast Gallery** Right **Kaupo Store**

Places to Eat and Shop

Uncle Harry's
Named after, and originally owned by, the late "Uncle" Harry Mitchell, this roadside stand (now run by Uncle's family) stocks fruit, snacks, and soft drinks. ◈ *Hāna Highway, just past the turn for Ke'anae • Map J3 • No regular days or hours*

Waianu Fruit Stand
In Uncle Harry's neighborhood, a somewhat larger and more modern place to stock up on goods for the rest of the drive. ◈ *Nr Ke'anae on the Hāna Highway • Map J3 • Open daily ... usually*

Tutu's Snack Shop
Down at Hāna Bay, Tutu's serves inexpensive local-style breakfasts and plate lunches. Maui's own luscious Roselani macadamia nut ice cream somehow tastes better here than anywhere else. ◈ *Map L4 • Mon–Sat 8am–4pm • $*

Paniolo Bar
A pleasant spot for a fulsome cocktail or a fruity afternoon snack; the exotic tropical concoctions can often double as both. ◈ *In the Hotel Hāna Maui • Map L4*

Ka'uiki
The award-winning dining room at Hotel Hāna-Maui offers Pacific Island cuisine, featuring fresh fish and locally grown produce. It has a majestic view of Hāna Bay. ◈ *Hotel Hāna-Maui • Map L4 • Hula performances Fri evenings • 248 8211 • $$$$$*

Hāna Ranch Restaurant
Opposite the bank and post office in what passes for the hub of Hāna town, the Ranch offers hearty servings of wholesome food in a fittingly rustic setting. ◈ *Map L4 • 270 5280 • $$$*

Hāna Coast Gallery
Charming Patrick Robinson has run this gallery for years and is extremely knowledgeable about the excellent local artists represented. Paintings, prints, furniture, jewelry, etc. ◈ *At the Hotel Hāna-Maui • Map L4 • 248 8636*

Hasegawa General Store
Immortalized in song, you really CAN get just about anything at Harry Hasegawa's wonderful, old-fashioned general store. A must-stop, even if you don't need anything. ◈ *5165 Hāna Highway • Map L4 • Mon–Sat 7am–7pm, Sun 8am–6pm*

Hāna Ranch Store
Hāna's other store focuses mostly on foodstuffs, including delicious roasted, ready-for-a-picnic chickens. ◈ *Up the hill and across the road from Hasegawa's, Hāna • Map L4 • 7am–7:30pm daily*

Kaupo Store
"In the middle of nowhere" is one way to describe the whereabouts of this convenience store and "museum." Eight miles past Seven Pools ('Ohe'o Gulch) heading toward 'Ulupalakua is the actual location. ◈ *Map J6 • No regular hours*

Note: *Unless otherwise stated, all restaurants accept credit cards and serve vegetarian meals; for price categories see p89*

Left **Mule ride** Center **Ili'ili'opae Heiau** Right **Lāna'i City house and Cook Island pines**

Moloka'i and Lāna'i

THERE ARE NO STOP LIGHTS on Moloka'i, and that should tell you quite a lot about this serene and beautiful place. Everyone knows everyone else, and the pace of life is much slower than on all the other islands except, perhaps, for Lāna'i. Moloka'i's population of less than 7,000 congregate around the principal town of Kaunakakai. The island offers spectacular scenery, quiet island life, and is just a 15-minute flight from Maui. Lāna'i is even smaller – just 13 miles wide and 18 miles long, with a population of less than 3,000. It has served as a penal colony, ranch, pineapple plantation, and now as a luxury resort destination. The idyll can be reached via a short ferry crossing from Lahaina.

🔟 Sights Molokai

1. Kaunakakai
2. Kamakou & Mo'omomi Nature Preserves
3. St. Joseph's Church
4. Hālawa Valley
5. Moloka'i Museum and Cultural Center
6. Kalaupapa Peninsula
7. Kaunolū
8. Munro Trail
9. Luahiwa Petroglyph Field
10. Garden of the Gods

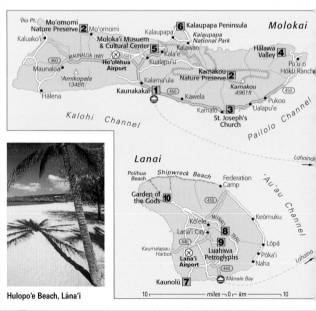

Hulopo'e Beach, Lāna'i

Left **Kaunakakai Harbor** Right **Moa'ula Falls**

Kaunakakai

The commercial and population center of Moloka'i, Kaunakakai was once a canoe landing for access to fishing grounds, and the beach was exclusively for the recreation of chiefly families. In the 1800s it became a plantation town – first sugar and then pineapple – in the early 1900s. This charming one-street town has changed little in the last 70 years. ✎ Map C6

Kamakou & Mo'omomi Nature Preserves

Kamakou Preserve lies near the summit of Moloka'i's highest mountain. This lush rain forest is home to more than 250 species of Hawaiian plants – 219 of them found nowhere else in the world – and a unique array of birds, such as the Moloka'i thrush (oloma'o) and the Moloka'i creeper (kākā-wahie). The seemingly barren dunes of Mo'omomi shelter rare coastal species, Hawaiian archaeological sites, and native shorebirds, like sanderlings and plovers. Both preserves are open to the public, but each is remote and access requires a four-wheel-drive vehicle. ✎ Map D6 & B5 • To visit first call the Nature Conservancy of Hawai'i: 553 5236

St. Joseph's Church

Located off of Highway 450 at mile marker 11, this small rural church was built in 1876 by Belgian priest Father Damien, who was best known for his work at the Hansen's disease settlement on Kalaupapa (see pp26–7). Standing outside, and often draped with flower lei in tribute, is a statue of Damien. The door to the church is always unlocked, and visitors are welcome to enter. ✎ Map D6

Hālawa Valley

The extreme eastern tip of Moloka'i is marked by the Hālawa Valley. It lies at the end of a scenic winding road, and an overlook at the valley's entrance offers a breathtaking view of the 250-ft Moa'ula Falls cascading down the mountain and the freshwater stream running to the ocean. Take the road down into the valley, but do not cross the inlet as the other side is private property. ✎ Map D5

St. Joseph's Church

Left **Moloka'i Museum and Cultral Center** Right **Kalaupapa Peninsula**

Moloka'i Museum and Cultural Center

Also known as the Sugar Mill Museum, this 19th-century industrial building was the work of R.W. Meyer, a German immigrant engineer. When the mill first turned in 1878, it used real horsepower and a steam engine to crush and process sugar cane. The building has been lovingly and beautifully restored, and now exhibitions are held regularly. You can also take a self-guided tour through the mill. ⊗ *Kala'e Highway • Map C5 • Mon–Sat 10am–2pm • Adm*

Kalaupapa Peninsula

Cut off from the rest of the island by sheer cliffs and surrounded by the ocean on three sides, this isolated peninsula became the place where Hansen's disease (leprosy) sufferers were quarantined. It's now a spectacular National Park encompassing more than 10,000 acres of land and water. *(See pp26–7.)*

Kaunolū

Located on the southwest shore of Lāna'i, this deserted precontact Hawaiian village was once a vigorous fishing community. There are stone foundations of

Hawaiian Fishponds

Early Hawaiians constructed fishponds as an early form of fish farming. An encircling wall of stone or coral was given gatelike openings to circulate fresh seawater into the ponds, while keeping predators out. When mature fish were needed for food, they were harvested by net.

more than 100 homes, storerooms, garden walls, and burial sites, as well as the stone platform of the Halulu Heiau temple, the ruins of a canoe *hale* (house), a large fishing shrine, and a platform of the cliff-side home of Kamehameha Nui (I). Signs are dotted around with information about the sites and ruins. ⊗ *Map L3*

Munro Trail

Up, up from Kō'ele through mountain grasslands, where rain forests of pine, ironwood, and

Garden of the Gods

Luahiwa Petroglyph

eucalyptus line the mountain's backbone ridge to the island's summit, Lāna'ihale, the Munro Trail offers spectacular views of nearby islands. The trail is named in honor of former ranch manager George Munro, and it was he who planted the ridge and highlands with the Cook Island pine trees you can see today. The intent was to draw moisture from the passing clouds and provide an adequate watershed for the island. Foot or four-wheel drive vehicle are the best ways to travel the trail. ✪ *From Lana'i City, take the Keomuku Rd. and at mile marker 1 turn right on the first major gravel road, then take the left fork • Map L2*

Luahiwa Petroglyph Field
One of the most exciting and fascinating collections of petroglyphs in Hawai'i, Luahiwa is hard to find but, once there, easily viewed. Covering numerous boulders on the hillside, these well-preserved drawings, carved by early Hawaiians, represent men and women, family units, pets, canoes, and, possibly, a surfer. ✪ *At six tall pine trees on the Mānele Rd., turn left onto Ho'ike Rd., continue for a mile, then turn left again, and drive on for half a mile • Map L2*

Garden of the Gods
No verdant oasis of foliage and flowers, Garden of the Gods is an eerily beautiful, windswept landscape of red, purple, and ocher rocks, sculpted by the raging forces of nature into irregular pinnacles and buttes. Sunsets are particularly spectacular here. ✪ *Map K1*

A Moloka'i Day Trip

Morning

🕐 Take a leisurely drive – there's no other way on Moloka'i – to the spectacular **Hālawa Valley** on the island's far eastern end.

Begin in Kaunakakai with a breakfast of sweet bread from **Kanemitsu Bakery** *(see p102)*. Stock up in town with snacks and drinks for a picnic.

From **Kaunakakai**, take Route 450 heading east. Be sure to notice all the ancient fishponds still intact along the coastline. About 11 miles from Kaunakakai you'll see, in quick succession, **St. Joseph's** and then **Our Lady of Sorrows** *(p100)* – both built by Father Damien in the late 1800s. Step inside to experience the history.

The road to Hālawa is winding, narrow, and extraordinarily scenic. Take your time to enjoy it – pull over, stop for a picnic or a snack, or to snap some photos, and immerse yourself in the glorious surroundings and clean, fresh air.

Afternoon

Hālawa Valley is absolutely perfect: a high waterfall cascades into the stream that winds through the valley and eventually reaches the ocean. The base of the valley is a great place for a picnic if you haven't already eaten, or to kick back and feast on the views.

Once you've luxuriated in the tranquillity of the valley, retrace your journey back to Kaunakakai in time for an afternoon swim followed by dinner at **Hula Shores** *(see p102)*.

Left **Kapuāiwa Coconut Grove** Center **'Ualapu'e Fishpond** Right **Hulopo'e Beach**

🔟 Best of the Rest

1 Kapuāiwa Coconut Grove
A grove planted in the 1860s by King Kamehameha V. As well as providing shade for the king's sacred bathing pools, each of the 1,000 majestic, royal coconut palms represented a warrior in his mighty army. Only a few hundred of the beautiful palms still stand. ⦿ *Map C6*

2 'Ualapu'e Fishpond
East of Kaunakakai the coast is scalloped with more than 50 ancient fishponds, most visible from the road. Constructed in the 13th century for use by the *ali'i* (royalty), this pond was in use until it was damaged by a tsunami in 1960. ⦿ *Map D6*

3 Kalua'aha Church
This church, site of the first Protestant mission on Moloka'i, was completed in 1844. The building is open to the public. ⦿ *Map D6*

4 Our Lady of Sorrows Church
Beautifully silhouetted by the mountains, Our Lady of Sorrows is one of the churches established on the island by Father Damien *(see p27)*. ⦿ *Map D6*

5 'Ili'ili'opae Heiau
Moloka'i is famed throughout the islands for its religious practices and sorcery. 'Ili'ili'opae Heiau was the "school" for sorcerers – a very powerful 13th-century temple that was known for human sacrifice. ⦿ *Map D6*

6 Maunaloa
The fortunes of Maunaloa mirrored the rise and fall of the pineapple industry. Currently, the main street contains a few family-run stores. These are the last places for stocking up before heading to the beaches. ⦿ *Map A6*

7 Kane'apua Rock
The waters around this lava rock outcropping at the southern tip of Lāna'i are well known for excellent fishing. The ocean is often rough, though, and not good for swimming. ⦿ *Nr Kaunolu • Map L3*

8 Hulopo'e Beach
This palm-fringed, white sand beach is the classic picture of Hawai'i. A shallow pool blasted from the rock for the island's children provides easy viewing of tidepool life, the waves are usually mellow, and the snorkeling terrific. ⦿ *Map L3*

9 Keōmuku Village
Once a thriving sugar settlement, Keōmuku has been a ghost town since the early 20th century. Local lore blames the village's demise on the disruption of temple stones at Kahe'a heiau by railroad builders. ⦿ *Map M2*

10 Kānepu'u Reserve
The Native Hawaiian Dryland Forest at Kānepu'u is an area of rare plant life. Some 48 native species can be found here, including local relatives of the olive and persimmon. ⦿ *Map L2*

Left **Moloka'i Mule Ride** Center **Moloka'i Fish and Dive Co.** Right **The Challenge at Mānele**

 Moloka'i and Lāna'i Activities

Moloka'i Mule Ride
One of the most unusual adventures in Hawai'i, visitors ride mules down 1,700 ft of steep and winding trail to the remote settlement of Kalaupapa (see pp26–7). The entire tour takes a full day beginning at 8am. ✆ 1-800 567 7550, 567 6088 • www.muleride.com

Moloka'i Fish and Dive Co.
This is your one-stop shop for fixing up any activity that you can think of – from kayaking to biking, hiking to horseback riding, and archery to paintball.
✆ Kaunakakai: 553 5926

Moloka'i Off-Road Tours
One of the few companies offering guided tours on Moloka'i, with a choice of itineraries. Plan to spend at least half a day with your guide. ✆ 553 3369

Lāna'i Pine Sporting Clays
The enjoyment of hunting without harming a live animal is the appeal of sporting clays, especially with high-tech targets that actually mimic different animals and birds. ✆ 559 4600

Trilogy Excursions
This long-established pleasure boating company offers a range of on-the-water experiences, including sailing on a catamaran or cruising in a high-powered raft. You can snorkel, scuba, and kayak all year round, and watch whales in winter. ✆ Office: 180 Lahainaluna Rd., Lahaina, Maui • 661 4743

Lāna'i Pine Archery Range
All levels of archers can take aim at the bright red, yellow, and blue targets mounted on straw bales. Private and group lessons are also offered. ✆ 559 4600

The Experience at Kō'ele
Designed by golf great Greg Norman and architect Ted Robinson, this award-winning championship course presents challenging fairways, creative water features, and a demanding signature hole that drops 200 ft to a wooded gorge. ✆ Map L2 • 565 4653

The Challenge at Mānele
American golf legend Jack Nicklaus designed this awesome course, built on natural lava outcroppings overlooking the Mānele Bay Hotel, Hulopo'e Bay, and the Pacific Ocean. The 12th hole plays from a cliff 150 ft above the crashing surf and requires a demanding 200-yard tee shot across the ocean. ✆ Map L3 • 565 2222

The Stables at Kō'ele
Trail rides through woods, over hills, and across plains are offered, as are private lessons, children's rides, and a carriage tour. ✆ Map L2 • 565 4424

Spinning Dolphin Charters
The one and only choice for sport fishing excursions off Lāna'i. Spinning Dolphin offers half- and full-day charters for up to six people. ✆ 565 7676

Price Categories

Price categories include a three-course meal for one, a glass of house wine, and all unavoidable extra charges including tax.	**$** under $20
	$$ $20–$30
	$$$ $30–$45
	$$$$ $45–$60
	$$$$$ over $60

Left **Kanemitsu Bakery** Right **Lana'i City Grille**

🔟 Places to Eat

1 Kanemitsu Bakery
The bakery's famed French bread is stuffed with cream cheese, strawberry or blueberry jam, and cinnamon butter. ◈ *Ala Malama St., Kaunakakai • Map C6 • $*

2 Outpost Natural Food Store and Juice Bar
Quaint county-style store, selling natural foods and vitamins. A juice bar provides all-vegetarian burritos, salads, sandwiches, and smoothies. ◈ *Ala Malama St., Kaunakakai • Map C6 • Store Sun–Fri; Juice bar Mon–Fri • 553 3377 • $*

3 Moloka'i Pizza Café
Off the main drag – on the wharf road – this clean, well-lit little café offers pizza, pasta, sandwiches, and seafood. Nothing fancy, but all good. ◈ *Kaunakakai Place, Kaunakakai • Map C6 • $*

4 Hula Shores Restaurant
The ribs and coconut shrimp are fabulous. On Friday evenings, listen in as cowboys, grandmas, and everyone in between tunes up their 'ukulele and gets down for a good, ole fashioned *kanikapila* (Hawaiian jam session). ◈ *Hotel Moloka'i, Kamehameha V Highway, Kaunakakai • Map C6 • 553 5347 • $$$*

5 Paddler's Inn
Burgers, sandwiches, and plate lunches dominate the menu at this diner-style eatery. It also offers a Sunday brunch and nightly entertainment. ◈ *10 Mohala St., Kaunakakai • 553 5256 • Map C6 • $$*

6 Lana'i City Grille
Located in the quaint Hotel Lana'i, the menu here was created by Maui celebrity chef Bev Gannon. It features generous portions of fresh local fish and the signature rotisserie chicken. Live music Friday evenings. ◈ *Hotel Lana'i, 828 Lana'i Ave., Lana'i City • Map L2 • 565 7211 • $$$$$*

7 Blue Ginger Café
A throwback to simpler times, this casual eatery, for breakfast, lunch, dinner, and home-baked bread, is probably the most popular restaurant on the island with locals. ◈ *409 7th St., Lana'i City • Map L2 • 565 6363 • $*

8 Canoes
Big breakfasts, lunch specials such as fresh fish and baby back ribs, and considerable Hawaiian *aloha* (warmth). ◈ *Lana'i City • Map L2 • Closed Wed • 656 6537 • $$*

9 The Formal Dining Room at the Lodge
Local ingredients are transformed into edible works of art, and served in an elegant room. ◈ *Dinner only • Four Seasons Resort Lāna'i, The Lodge at Ko'ele • Jacket required • Map L2 • 565 7300 • $$$$$*

10 'Ihilani at Mānele Bay
A formal beachside restaurant, its menus change with availability of fresh ingredients. ◈ *Four Seasons Resort Lāna'i at Mānele Bay • Map L3 • Tue–Sat, dinner only • Jacket required • 565 7700 • $$$$$*

Note: *Unless otherwise stated, all restaurants accept credit cards and serve vegetarian meals*

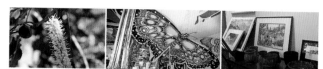

Left **Purdy's Macadamia Nut Farm** Center **Big Wind Kite Factory** Right **Heart of Lāna'i Art Gallery**

TOP 10 Shopping

1 Ala Malama Street
This is small-town U.S.A., Moloka'i style. On Saturdays, take a leisurely look at the farmers' market, which is also part swap meet, part social gathering. ◈ *Kaunankakai • Map C6*

2 Moloka'i Fine Arts Gallery
More than 140 Moloka'i artists, ranging from painters and photographers to wood-turners, fabric artists, and Moloka'i shell jewelry makers, are showcased at this gallery. ◈ *2 Kamoi St., Kaunakakai • Map C6*

3 Purdy's Macadamia Nut Farm
A small, one-acre family farm, with personal tours conducted by the Purdy family. Their macadamia trees produce luscious nuts, which you can taste in all stages of development. ◈ *Ho'olehua Homestead • Map B5 • Tue–Sat*

4 Coffees of Hawai'i
This plantation offers walking tours of its coffee processing and roasting operations twice a day. Brands produced on-site include Malulani, Muleskinner, and Moloka'i Princess. ◈ *Kualapu'u, central Moloka'i • Map C5*

5 Big Wind Kite Factory/ Plantation Gallery
You can buy handmade kites and windsocks, and view the owners' collection of drums, baskets, jewelry, and textiles. ◈ *120 Maunaloa Hwy., Maunaloa • Map A6*

6 Heart of Lāna'i Art Gallery
Hotel Lāna'i artist-in-residence Denise Hennig owns and operates this gallery. Stop by for one of her afternoon "Lāna'i-Kine" teas. ◈ *Lāna'i City • Map L2 • 565 7815 • Tue–Sat 2:30–4:30pm*

7 Gifts With Aloha
Owners Kim and Phoenix Dupree seek out unique, locally handmade art and craft items for their shop. You'll find gifts ranging from food produce to wooden vases, and soaps to books. ◈ *363 7th St., Lāna'i City • Map L2*

8 The Local Gentry
A clothing boutique that seems more suited to Honolulu than Lāna'i. But Genna Gentry's assortment of swimsuits, casual clothing, and chic evening wear is tailor-made for smart vacationers. ◈ *363 7th St., Lāna'i City • Map L2*

9 Dis 'n Dat Shop
In typically laid-back Lāna'i style, the owners of this whimsical shop, which specializes in merchandise to "enhance your home and your soul," decided to keep with the store's original name. ◈ *418 8th St., Lāna'i City • Map L2*

10 Richards Shopping Center
A true old-fashioned general store, there's a little bit of everything you might need here. In addition to groceries and sundries, you can stock up on fishing and camping gear, clothing, wine, and cold beer. ◈ *434 8th St. • Map L2*

STREETSMART

MAUI'S TOP 10

Left **Casual clothing** Center **Passenger aircraft** Right **Luxury liner**

Planning Your Visit

1 When to Visit
In terms of weather, Hawai'i is good to visit year round. May, June, September, and October are traditionally a bit slower than the height of winter and summer seasons, so better travel deals are often available during those months.

2 Passport and Visa Requirements for Foreign Visitors
Citizens from the EU, New Zealand, Australia, and Japan can spend up to 90 days in the U.S. without a visa, but they must register online with the Electronic System for Travel Authorization (ESTA) beforehand. You will also need a valid passport and a round-trip ticket. Canadian citizens need to show a valid passport. Visitors from other countries must contact their local U.S. embassy well in advance to obtain the relevant visa.

3 Customs/Agricultural Inspection
Foreign visitors may not bring food or plants of any kind into Hawai'i. Every piece of luggage or cargo leaving the islands is subject to an agricultural search. Only certain fruits and flowers may be taken out, so be sure to ask about this when purchasing such items.

4 Climate
Contrary to popular belief, Hawai'i does have seasons. Rain is common from Oct–Jan, and summer is much warmer than winter. Big surf arrives on north shores in winter; south swells delight surfers in summer. At sea level, temperatures average high 70s/low 80s in the day most of the year; night temperatures can go down to the 60s, occasionally the 50s in winter.

5 Electricity
Standard U.S. current is 110–120 volts. Non-U.S. appliances need a converter and plug adapter with two flat pins, but bear in mind many hotels already provide coffee makers, irons, and hair dryers.

6 Clothing
Hawai'i is a relaxed place. Shorts, tees, swimsuits, and casual evening wear is all that's really needed. Most restaurants don't have a formal dress code. A sweater or jacket is a good idea for cool evenings, and, if you plan to go Upcountry, you should take warm clothing.

7 Insurance
The cost of medical care is high throughout the U.S., including Hawai'i. If you have a mainland health insurance plan, you should check to see if it's accepted in Hawai'i. Otherwise, travel insurance is recommended.

8 Major Airlines
U.S. airlines are facing difficult times, and flight schedules and routes change frequently. United, American, and Delta Airlines all fly directly to Maui from mainland U.S.; many major airlines fly into Honolulu from the mainland, Europe, and Asia.

9 Enhanced Security
Although Hawai'i is a safe place, due to fears of terrorism, airport security has been enhanced. Items like pocketknives and scissors must be packed in checked luggage. Carry-on liquids and gels must fit in one clear, small sized plastic bag. Try to reach the airport an hour early for inter-island flights.

10 Cruise Lines
Crystal Cruises, Princess Cruises, and Royal Caribbean have ships that stop in Hawai'i as part of wider itineraries. Norwegian Cruise Lines operates vessels through the Hawaiian islands.

Directory

United Airlines
www.ual.com

American Airlines
www.aa.com

Delta Airlines
www.delta.com

Crystal Cruises
www.crystalcruises.com

Princess Cruises
www.princess.com

Royal Caribbean
www.royalcaribbean.com

Norwegian Cruise Lines www.ncl.com

Previous pages **Plantation Inn** *(see p119)*

Left **Maui Visitors Bureau** Center **Magazines** Right **Locals**

🔟 Sources of Information

1 Maui Visitors Bureau

The Maui Visitors Bureau is the official source of visitor information *(see directory)*, though it doesn't make recommendations. It oversees similar agencies on Moloka'i and Lāna'i.

2 Magazines

Hana Hou! the Hawaiian Airlines in-flight magazine is published six times a year and includes dining, shopping, and entertainment ideas. *HONOLULU* is Hawai'i's only major regional magazine and is great if you're looking for insider information, although the coverage definitely favors Honolulu/O'ahu. Both can be accessed online.

3 Newspapers

The Maui News is Maui's only daily newspaper. It's available each day by about 6am. *The Lahaina News* is a weekly and focuses on West Maui news. *Maui Weekly* and *Maui Time Weekly* are free publications. Look for them at the airport, markets, and other retail locations. Both big dailies, *The Honolulu Advertiser* and *Honolulu Star-Bulletin*, both morning papers, are distributed statewide.

4 Websites

Virtually every hotel chain, activities seller, and even most restaurants now have their own websites. They are easily accessed via any search engine. The Maui Visitors Bureau site also offers links to many individual visitor attractions.

5 Suggested Reading

James Michener's *Hawai'i* is considered by many a "must-read" for visitors. It is certainly epic in scope and an entertaining, if not precisely accurate, historical novel. Shoal of Time by Gavan Daws, *Hawai'i's History by Hawai'i's Queen* by Queen Liliu'okalani, and *Hawaiian Mythology* by Martha Beckwith are all excellent choices.

6 Visitor Channel TV

Paradise TV (Channel 7) broadcasts visitor information in a relaxed, "advertorial" format 24 hours a day. There are programs about dining, beaches, golf, shopping, and more.

7 Free Visitor Publications

You will be deluged by dozens of free visitor publications as soon as you arrive at any airport in Hawai'i. Many are chock full of discount coupons and free offers. Bear in mind that most publications cover only the places that advertise with them.

8 Concierge

Your hotel concierge is potentially one of the very best sources of insider information. They are, of course, island residents, and many know every nook and cranny of Maui – where to get the best noodles and find that vintage piece of Hawaiiana you simply must have. Remember to tip them well if the advice is good.

9 Talk to Locals

Hawai'i is known for having some of the world's friendliest locals, and most love to share their knowledge of their hometown. Talk to waiters and waitresses, the bartender, the supermarket cashier, and the person who sells you your very first aloha shirt. You're sure to learn secrets not available in any guidebook!

10 Activity Desks

There are activity desks in hotel lobbies, shopping malls, and on the street in Lahaina and Kīhei. The salespeople are usually very knowledgeable and can make all kinds of helpful recommendations.

Directory

Maui Visitors Bureau
- 1-800 525 6284 (toll-free)
- www.visitmaui.com

Magazine and Newspaper Websites
- www.hanahou.com
- www.honolulu magazine.com
- www.mauinews.com

Left **Interisland passenger aircraft** Center **Interisland ferry** Right **Shuttle bus**

🔟 Arriving & Getting Around Maui

1 Interisland Flights
Mokulele Airlines, Go!, and Hawaiian Airlines fly daily between the major islands. Island Air and Pacific Wings fly routes, like Kahului to Moloka'i, Lāna'i, and Hāna.

2 Rental Cars
There's lots of choice, but essentially it's between international companies, such as Hertz and Avis, or local businesses like Word of Mouth. The latter rent used vehicles to keep costs low.

3 Bicycles, Mopeds, and Motorcycles
Most of the rental firms specializing in two-wheeled vehicles are located in the Lahaina/Kā'anapali area. Bikes and mopeds tend to be used just for getting around town.

4 Shuttles, Taxis, and Ferries
SpeediShuttle provides transport between the Kahului Airport and the resort hotels at Wailea and Kā'anapali (fares approx $30 per person). Taxis, available by booking in advance, are expensive. There is a ferry service between Lahaina and Moloka'i and Lāna'i.

5 Rules of the Road
Seatbelts for everyone and approved car seats for children under three are mandatory. Right turns are permitted at a stop sign or red light after stopping, but pedestrians always have right of way.

6 Guided Tours
Robert's Hawai'i and Pleasant Hawaiian Holidays are the two largest land tour companies offering a variety of tours. Most popular are tours to the summit of Haleakalā and to Hāna.

7 Beach Access
All beaches in Hawai'i are public, but they often border private land. Watch for Public Beach Access signs, prominently displayed all around the coasts, and follow the path to the beach.

8 Maui Buses
Nine public transit bus routes serve central, west, south, and up-country Maui. Rides are $1; no transfers given.

9 Airport
Kahului Airport is nicely located in the center of the island. It's a small, friendly, and manageable place, just a few minutes away from the large retail centers of Kahului and quaint Wailuku town, about 25 minutes from Wailea, and about 40 minutes from the Kā'anapali resort area.

10 Local Etiquette
Local people are rarely in a hurry, and since most roads are two lanes only, it's best to simply adapt to the easygoing pace.

Directory

Interisland Airlines
- Mokulele Airlines 866 260 7070; www.mokuleleairlines.com
- Go! 888 435 9462; www.iflygo.com
- Hawaiian Airlines 800 367 5320; www.hawaiianair.com
- Island Air 800 652 6541
- Pacific Wings 888 575 4546; www.pacificwings.com

Car Rental
- Avis Rent A Car 800 831 2847; www.avis.com
- Hertz 800 654 3011; www.hertz.com
- Word of Mouth Rent-A-Used-Car 800 533 5929; www.mauirentacar.com

Bicycles, Mopeds, Motorcycles
- West Maui Cycles 808 661 9005
- Maui Harley-Davidson 808 877 7368

Shuttles, Taxis, Buses, Ferries
- SpeediShuttle 808 242 7777
- Maui Bus www.co.maui.hi.us/bus/
- Maui Central Cab 808 244 7278
- Sunshine Cabs of Maui 879 2220
- Lāna'i Passenger Ferry 808 661 3756
- Moloka'i Ferry 808 667 6165, 662 3355

Guided Tours
- Robert's Hawai'i 800 831 5541
- Pleasant Holidays 800 342 1566

If calling from within Maui, drop the 808 prefix on the phone numbers listed here

Left **Local vegetable stand** Center **Reservation discounts** Right **Visitor publications**

🔟 Budget Tips

1 Rent a Condo
Generally speaking, condominiums are less expensive than hotel rooms. Condo rentals are available all over West and South Maui and range from studios to three bedroom apartments. They're almost universally well maintained and equipped.

2 Eat In
The cost of dining out can easily rack up, so eating in is the obvious alternative, especially if you're renting a condo. Throughout south, west, and central Maui, there are lots of supermarkets, grocery stores, and farmers' markets where the fixings for a great meal can be easily found.

3 Ask about Discounts
Hotels, restaurants, and activity desks often offer discounts, especially during the slower months (May, June, September, October). For example, restaurants routinely offer "early bird" specials for folks who like to dine before the prime 6:30–8pm slot. Late night specials are also common, though less well advertised.

4 Plan Well Before You Travel
Virtually every airline, many hotels, even some car rental companies offer better prices to travelers who book well in advance. It's also a good idea to check out restaurants and activities – many have websites – before arriving to avoid price surprises. Some advance research also allows you to comparison shop for things like whale watching and other costly activities.

5 Use Visitor Coupons
When you arrive at any airport in Hawai'i, you will see racks and racks of free visitor publications. Every one of them has coupons for discounts on restaurant meals and activities. If you have the time and the inclination to peruse the pages, the savings can be substantial.

6 Frequent Flyer and Corporate Discounts
Frequent flyer miles can be used for both free or upgraded air travel on all the major U.S. airlines. If you are a member of a national organization such as AARP (for the over 50s) or work for a large corporation, ask about discounts. You may find that your company ID card can save you money!

7 Book a Package Tour
Package tours are always less expensive than purchasing air and ground transportation and accommodations separately; any good travel agent will have lots to choose from. But even if you do choose to book your own trip, interisland package tours (from local companies like Pleasant Island Holidays and Robert's Hawai'i) are an affordable way to experience another island.

8 Shop the Internet
The Internet has become a fantastic resource for excellent travel deals. The big, discount travel sites (Orbitz, Expedia, Hotels.com) always have reasonable prices on air fares and hotel rooms. Many of the major airlines also offer special Internet fares, and some hotels have discounted rates that are only available online.

9 Travel Off-Season
Hawai'i is most expensive during the winter months when travelers from cold climes swoop down upon these sundrenched, tropical islands. The summer months (July and August) are family travel time, since children are out of school. This leaves May, June, September, and October for the bargain hunters.

10 Book a Non-Ocean View Room
Oceanfront rooms are the most expensive accommodations in Hawai'i. Next come ocean view rooms and then partial ocean view rooms. In high-rise hotels, the upper floors are also priced at a premium. Booking a mountain or garden room view could save you hundreds of dollars on your accommodations bill.

Left **Cash point** Center left **Pay phone** Center right **Postal stamps** Right **Newspapers**

Streetsmart

⁧🔟⁩ Banking & Communications

1 Banks

Bank of Hawai'i and First Hawaiian Bank are Hawai'i's largest, with branches throughout the islands, some of them inside supermarkets. In general, all banks are open: Mon–Thu 8:30am–3pm or 4pm, Fri 8:30am–6pm. Some branches have Saturday hours.

2 Credit Cards

VISA and MasterCard are accepted almost universally except by the smallest stores and roadside stands. American Express, Discover, Diner's Club, and JCB (a Japanese card) are accepted at most places but check first.

3 Travelers' Checks

By far the safest form of money, travelers' checks in U.S. currency are accepted virtually everywhere. Change is given in cash. Lost or stolen travelers checks are easily replaced.

4 Telephone Calls

With the extraordinary propensity of cell phones, public phones are fast disappearing. If you can find one, a local call will cost 50 cents. Many hotels offer free local calls. Interisland calls are deemed long distance, and numbers must be preceded by dialing 1-808.

5 Postal Services

A postcard will cost you 28 cents postage, a standard letter to any U.S. address 44 cents. Hotels will often post your mail for you, but there are also post offices in every town. Opening hours are generally: 8:30am–4:30pm Mon–Fri, with short morning hours at some branches on Saturdays.

6 Newspapers and Magazines

The best place to purchase mainland newspapers and a wide array of magazines is Borders at Maui Marketplace in Kahului *(see p75)*. *The Maui News* is Maui's only daily paper; *The Honolulu Advertiser* and *Honolulu Star-Bulletin* are statewide dailies. *Maui Nō Ka 'Oi* is the only Maui-specific magazine; *HONOLULU* is Hawai'i's regional monthly magazine, available on all newsstands. For more on newspapers and magazines, see p107.

7 Television and Radio

In addition to the myriad U.S. television channels, Maui has several local access stations. One of these, Paradise TV, is the visitor channel. Its programming provides an overview of the island, activities, shopping, and restaurants. Fans of every music genre should find something on the radio dial to satisfy their tastes, but if you want to listen to what the locals listen to, try KPOA, 93.5 FM for the best in island sounds.

8 "Coconut Wireless"

This is Hawai'i's version of "hearing it through the grapevine." Talk to as many locals as you can; you'll be pleasantly surprised at how willing most are to share the island's secrets.

9 Internet Access

Most hotel rooms and condos are equipped with Internet access. And most of the larger hotels have business centers with equipment to stay in touch with the office. Internet service is also available at several cafés.

10 Hawai'i Time

Unlike the U.S. mainland, Hawai'i does not subscribe to Daylight Savings Time, meaning that island time remains constant throughout the year. From Oct–Apr, Hawai'i is two hours behind the U.S. West Coast; from Apr–Oct three hours.

Directory

Banks
• Bank of Hawai'i 888 643 3888
• First Hawaiian Bank 808 873 2234

Lost Cards & Checks
• *American Express* 800 528 4800 (cards), 800 221 7282 (travelers' checks)
• *VISA* 800 336 8472
• *MasterCard* 800 826 2181

Left **Use sunscreen at the beach** Center **Beach warning signs** Right **Carry water when hiking**

TOP 10 Things to Avoid

1 Sunburn
Everyone is at risk of sunburn in the tropics. It's important to apply sunscreen often, most especially after swimming. A hat and sunglasses are good accessories, too. If you're especially fair, you should wear light, long-sleeved shirts and long pants when you're in the sun. Parents should be particularly careful with young children. Be vigilant on cloudy days, too – those ultraviolet rays get through the clouds.

2 Flash Floods
During heavy rains, Hawai'i's rivers are occasionally susceptible to flash floods. It's best not to venture out on hikes or unfamiliar drives during heavy rains. Hawai'i radio and television stations always announce flash flood watches and warnings; you can also check recorded national weather forecasts by calling 877 5111.

3 Heat Stroke
Although blessed with cooling trade winds most days of the year, temperatures can easily reach into the 90s, especially in summer. It's always advisable to stay out of the sun from 11am until 2pm when, obviously, the sun is at its highest point over the islands. Wearing light-colored clothing and drinking lots of water are also recommended.

4 Dehydration
With heat and sun comes the possibility of dehydration. Always carry water with you, whether you're going for a drive, venturing out on a hike, or just relaxing at the beach. Drink often and drink plenty.

5 Bites and Stings
Scorpions and centipedes are Hawai'i's most troublesome insect pests. It is unlikely that you will run into either but, if you do get stung, get medical attention as quickly as possible. Mosquitoes are more bothersome than dangerous, and can be controlled with commercial repellants.

6 Trespassing
It's not difficult to accidentally wander onto private property, especially when hiking or going to the beach. Watch for No Trespassing signs, and always use the proper public beach accesses. You may see the word *Kapu* on signs, which is loosely translated as "forbidden."

7 Littering
The physical beauty of the islands is most certainly one of the main reasons visitors are so drawn to them. Nothing is more jarring to that beauty than litter strewn along beaches, hiking paths, and streets. There's no shortage of litter bins for food wrappers,

cigarette stubs etc., so make use of them. (*Mahalo*, often printed on the bins, means thank you.)

8 Removing Natural Objects
Traditional Hawaiians believe that everything – every stone, every shell, every plant – has both a life and a place of its own. So feel free to look, enjoy, and touch natural objects, but refrain from removing anything from its "home."

9 Jellyfish
Hawaiian waters are susceptible to invasions of jellyfish – both box jellyfish and Portuguese man-of-war – usually about a week after a full moon. Local radio and television stations are very reliable in reporting these incursions. Jellyfish stings can be painful and, if one is allergic, quite dangerous. The best way to treat them is with meat tenderizer (available at any supermarket) or, indeed, urine.

10 Sharp Coral
The islands are surrounded by reefs of coral, much of it very sharp. It can cause nasty cuts that are susceptible to infection, as coral is a living organism. Clean out a coral cut quickly and completely, treat it with an antiseptic, and keep it covered up. If a coral cut does get infected, it should be treated by a medical practitioner.

Left **Ocean safety sign** Center **Keep your rental car locked** Right **Sharp coral beneath the waves**

Safety Tips

1 Ocean Safety
With care and common sense, it's easy to enjoy the gorgeous Pacific that surrounds the islands, but it's as well to remember that strong currents, big waves, undertow, sharp coral, and potentially dangerous sea creatures are all natural parts of Hawai'i's environment. Also, many beaches are not staffed by lifeguards. A red flag on the beach indicates strong currents, and posted signs will alert you to other possible dangers.

2 Medical Emergencies
As in the rest of the U.S., dialing 911 in Hawai'i will put you in touch with the emergency services. Maui Memorial Medical Center in Wailuku is the island's major hospital, and there are clinics in all major towns. In addition, the resort hotels have doctors on call.

3 Climate & Quakes
Blessed with a near perfect climate all year round, Hawai'i is, however, susceptible to extreme weather and natural disasters, most notably hurricanes (from June to November), tidal waves, and earthquakes. Earthquakes are not uncommon but are usually benign. Maui's Upcountry district from Makawao at the 1500-ft level of Mt. Haleakalā to the summit at 10,023 ft

is cool throughout the year and can be very cold at the higher elevations, especially in the winter.

4 Smart Hiking
Good shoes are recommended, especially for serious hikers; rainforest trails can get very muddy and slick. Carry plenty of water and snacks and be absolutely sure of your route before you begin. Never hike alone and make sure someone – even if it's your hotel concierge – knows where you're going and what time you're expected back.

5 Sun Sense
The sun in the tropics is stronger than anywhere else, even when it doesn't feel that way and even when the sky is overcast. Using sunscreen is an absolute must, as is reapplication throughout the day. Fair-skinned people should wear a hat and light-colored, long-sleeved clothing where possible. And remember to continue drinking water throughout the day.

6 Avoiding Car Theft
Even in paradise, theft is a problem, and tourists' rental cars are often the targets. Obviously, lock your car when you park, even if you leave it for just a few moments, and never leave anything of value on view; in fact, whenever possible, keep valuables with you.

7 Water
All hotels and most other accommodations have filtration systems so the tap water is perfectly safe unless otherwise indicated. Bottled water is handy for carrying with you on day trips. Never drink from streams, ponds, rivers, waterfalls, or freshwater pools.

8 Lock Your Doors
Hawai'i is a very casual and, in general, an extremely safe place. All the same, you should always lock your hotel room or condo. And don't forget to make sure any balcony doors are secure before you go out – they allow very easy access.

9 Valuables
The very best way to ensure the safety of your valuables is to leave them at home. Every hotel has either in-room safes or lock boxes on the property to store cash, jewelry, traveler's checks, and other treasures. And it's never a good idea to take anything of value to the beach with you.

10 Snorkeling and Scuba Safety
The buddy system ensures that you never dive alone and that you share responsibility for your safety. Full scuba instruction is widely available, but even if you're already a certified diver, familiarize yourself with the underwater terrain before any excursion.

Left **Local Craft stand** Center **Discount store** Right **Evening dining**

☺10 Shopping and Dining Tips

1 Opening Times

Large shopping centers are open, in general, Mon–Sat 9am–9pm; Sunday hours are usually shorter. Some supermarkets and convenience stores stay open 24 hours. Most retail stores are open on U.S. holidays (with the possible exception of Christmas Day and New Year's Day) and Hawai'i state holidays, such as Prince Kūhiō Day (Mar 26) and King Kamehameha Day (Jun 11).

2 Alcohol and Smoking Laws

The legal drinking age in Hawai'i is 21. The age limit applies, as well, to buying alcoholic drinks – including beer and wine – at retail outlets. Smoking is now prohibited in stores, restaurants, bars, and other public spaces, including outdoor dining areas.

3 Early Bird Specials

Not surprisingly, everyone wants to dine at sunset. In order to encourage pre-sunset dinner reservations, many restaurants offer "early bird specials" (see p109).

4 Sales Tax

There's general excise tax – 4.167% at the time of writing – on everything, without exception, in Hawai'i. That includes food – whether a restaurant meal or groceries from the market – all retail goods (even medicine), and all services.

5 Evening Dining Hours

"Early to bed, early to rise" is the credo throughout the Aloha State. Don't be surprised if the restaurant on which you have your romantic heart set for a late night dinner stops serving at 8:30 or 9pm. The same is true of breakfast and lunch – many local folks take their lunch break at 11 or even 10:30am.

6 Casual and Formal Dining

There are, literally, no restaurants on Maui that require anything fancier than a shirt with a collar and footwear of some kind; there are only a handful that would frown on shorts and sandals. Lāna'i has a few more airs and graces, and two of its top restaurants require formal dress (see p102).

7 Tipping

Most of Maui's residents work in the visitor industry and depend on tips to supplement their wages, so generosity is greatly appreciated. Restaurant tips should be at least 15% of the total bill. Parking valets should be tipped $1–$2; luggage handlers at least $2 per bag. And if you avail yourself of the service, you should also tip your hotel concierge.

8 Shop at the Local Stores

You'll save money on souvenirs, resort wear, even groceries if you shop where the islanders go. Local favorite Long's Drugs has shops in Kahului, Kīhei, and Lahaina, and is great for macadamia nuts, coffee, and lots more. There are farmers' markets scattered throughout the island and there's a big swap meet in Kahului every Saturday morning, with excellent buys on flowers, local produce, and crafts.

9 Cheap Eats

Maui's ethnic restaurants serve delicious food at low prices. These places are centered, for the most part, in Wailuku and offer Vietnamese, Chinese, Japanese, Mexican, and local-style food. At more expensive restaurants, sharing several appetizers is a great way to sample dishes without paying a fortune. (For more budget tips, see p109.)

10 Check When Buying Souvenirs

Unfortunately, much of what passes for made in Hawai'i goods are actually manufactured in China, Taiwan, or the Philippines. A "Made-in-Hawai'i" label may, indeed, be fake. Always ask to be sure you're getting the genuine article when you're shopping.

Left **Kayaking** Center **Hiking** Right **A** ranch *paniolo* (cowboy)

🔟 Specialty Tours

Eco Tours
Maui Eco-Adventures offers daily hikes and kayak tours with very experienced and knowledgeable guides into less-traveled areas of the island, such as Haleakalā Crater and Hāna.

Hiking
The guides at Hike Maui share their knowledge of the island's ethno-botany, geology, culture, and history on hikes that could take you to Hāna's waterfalls, West Maui's rain forest, or the lava fields of the south.

Bicycle Tours
Aloha Bicycle Tours organizes a great ride along the scenic Upcountry road to the Tedeschi Winery. Twenty-four-speed bikes, jackets and gloves, luxury van tour support, continental breakfast, lunch, and wine tasting all included.

Cave Exploration
Maui Cave Adventures in Hāna takes novice and experienced spelunkers into Ka'elekū Caverns, an underground network of cool lava tubes with cavernous chambers (some 40 ft high). Gloves, flashlights, and hardhats are provided.

Jeep Tours
Maui's only Jeep guided tour company, Hidden Adventure, offers personalized full and half day four-wheel-drive adventures to explore dense rain forests,

colorful lava caves, windswept bluffs, and hidden bays. "Adventure" and "family" itineraries are offered; maximum of four people per vehicle.

Horse Riding
Mendes Ranch & Trail Rides offers two-and-a-half-hour narrated trails through rolling pastures into West Maui's rain forest, down the mountain to taro patches, and along Waihe'e Valley to the ocean.

Paragliding
Harnessed into a wing and lifted by air currents, pilots can float above the spectacular landscape around Haleakalā. Proflyght has the guidance and the gear to allow you to take off on your own or fly tandem with an instructor.

Scuba Diving
About 25% of the marine life in the clear waters off the island are unique to Hawai'i. To see those species and more, Mike Severns Diving takes small groups of certified divers to less crowded areas, such as Molokini.

Kayak Tours
Keli'i's two-and-half hour tour, for all skill levels, begins at Makena Landing and paddles leisurely along the coast to a snorkelling stop. Experienced guides provide instruction and accompany paddlers on the trip (eight paddlers per guide).

Blue Water Rafting
These fast, inflatable but stable, powered boats are ideal for skimming across the ocean. The Molokini Express Tour takes you to the sunken crater, where you can drift leisurely, snorkel, or explore the perimeter of the rim.

Directory

Maui Eco-Adventures
808 661 7720
www.ecomaui.com

Hike Maui
808 879 5270
www.hikemaui.com

Aloha Bicycle Tours
808 249 0911
www.mauibike.com

Maui Cave Adventures
808 248 7308
www.mauicave.com

Hidden Adventure Jeep Tours
808 264 1423 www. mauijeeptours.com

Mendes Ranch & Trail Rides
808 871 5222
www.mendesranch.com

Proflyght
808 874 5433 www. paraglidehawaii.com

Mike Severns Diving
808 879 6596 www. mikesevernsdiving.com

Keli'i's Kayak Tours
808 874 7652
www.keliiskayak.com

Molokini Express Tours
808 879 7238 www. bluewaterrafting.com

For more advice on water sports and other outdoor activities see pp40–49

Left **Young vacationers** Center **Disabled parking** Right **Laundromat**

TOP 10 Accommodation Tips

1 Traveling with Children

Hawai'i is an extremely family-friendly place. You'll see the word *keiki* (child) everywhere: restaurants offer *keiki* menus, and the resort hotels have *keiki* programs to keep the kids busy while the adults relax. In most hotels, small children can stay in their parents' room at no extra charge. Condos are a good, less expensive choice for families.

2 Visitors with Disabilities

Hawai'i is excellent for travelers with disabilities. Due in large part to the ADA (Americans with Disabilities Act), hotels, restaurants, and attractions provide wheelchair ramps, special parking places, and accessible restrooms. Braille translations of elevator button panels and other important signs are commonplace.

3 Hidden Extras

Accommodations are subject to both a 4.167% sales tax and up to 9.25% room tax so be prepared to find this additional 13.41% on your bill. Most hotels charge more than the standard rate for phone calls, faxes, and Internet access. Daily parking charges are also common.

4 Rates

At the low end of the spectrum are campsite permits and at the high end are luxury resort suites, villas, and bungalows. Mid-price hotel rooms are about $250 a night and $200 a night for a one-bedroom condo. Inns and B&Bs often have lovely rooms for $100 to $150 a night.

5 Packages

Travel agents and tour companies offer lots of packages that typically include air and ground transportation and accommodations; some even include interisland travel, activities, and some meals. Package deals change frequently, so best to inquire when you're ready to book your trip.

6 Deciphering Local Descriptions

When booking a room, bear in mind that only "oceanfront" means you will have a panoramic view of the blue Pacific. And you will, of course, pay a premium for that. "Partial ocean view" and "ocean view" are other common descriptions.

7 Spas

There is nothing so relaxing as spending a day, or even a few hours, at a spa – especially when it's in a tropical setting. Maui's resort hotels have spas offering body treatments, massage, facials, and fitness facilities. Non-guests are welcome to book spa services and use the facilities for a fee. For opulent grandeur, try the Spa Grande at the Grand Wailea; for low-key tranquillity and especially skilled practitioners, try the Spa Kea Lani at the Fairmont Kea Lani.

8 Reservation Services

Most of the resort hotels are part of international chains, and reservations can easily be made online. Travel agents can book almost any other accommodations available. Many hotels, condos, inns, and B&Bs have their own websites and accept reservations directly. The Maui Visitors Bureau can also help (see p107).

9 Tipping

Tipping hotel personnel is not required, but it is the done thing. Averages are $2–$3 a day for housekeepers, $1–$2 for parking valets, $1–$2 per piece of luggage for baggage handlers, and 15% for room service servers. Most guests tip the concierge as well, if they use their services.

10 Laundry and Dry Cleaning

All the resort hotels offer laundry and dry cleaning services, but prices tend to be higher than those at home. Condo complexes usually have coin-op laundries on site; it will cost a few dollars per load to wash and dry. Additional coin-operated laundromats are scattered throughout the island.

Left **Hyatt Regency Maui Resort & Spa** Center **Four Seasons Resort** Right **Hotel Hāna-Maui**

TOP 10 Luxury Resort Hotels and Spas

1 Hyatt Regency Maui Resort & Spa

Maui's first "fantasy resort" is located at the Lahaina end of Kā'anapali Beach and is still going strong after more than 25 years. The lush grounds, fantastic swimming pool (with a bar), swinging bridge, amazing art, variety of dining choices, luxurious spa, and upscale shopping arcade all contribute to the experience. ✪ Kā'anapali • Map B2 • 661 1234 • www.maui hyatt.com • $$$$$

2 The Westin Maui

Cascading waterfalls, an opulent lobby, and 55,000 sq ft of interconnected pools. Rooms are well appointed, with the chain's own Heavenly Beds, which promise you won't make it past the second page of your book. ✪ Kā'anapali • Map B2 • 667 2525 • www. westinmaui.com • $$$$$

3 Sheraton Maui

Kā'anapali's first ever luxury resort hotel is now looking a little dated, but it still has one of the best locations in Maui. Almost all of the 510 rooms face the ocean, and furnishings are reminiscent of old Hawai'i, utilizing bamboo, rattan, and kapa designs. The beach is noted for having phenomenal snorkelling, especially around Keka'a (see p66). ✪ Kā'anapali • Map B2 • 661 0031 • www.sheraton-maui.com • $$$$$

4 Royal Lahaina Resort

Located on an exclusive stretch of Kā'anapali Beach, this resort is set on sprawling tropical lawns and gardens. It has superb tennis facilities, including 11 paved courts and tournament seating. There is a nightly luau. ✪ Kā'anapali • Map B2 • 661 3611 • www. hawaiihotels.com • $$$$$

5 The Ritz-Carlton Kapalua

The activities of Hawaiian cultural specialist Clifford Nae'ole set this hotel apart and afford guests a chance to take in Hawaiian culture. The entire property, including all 463 rooms, amenities, restaurants, and spa, underwent a $180 million renovation in 2008. ✪ Kapalua • Map C1 • 808 669 6200 • www.ritz carlton.com • $$$$$

6 Wailea Point Village

Oceanfront condominiums on tropically landscaped grounds, with a gated entrance, heated pools, and all the amenities you would expect from a highend property. No credit cards accepted. ✪ 2439 S. Kihei Rd. • Map E5 • 879 7233 • www.waileapoint. com • $$$$$

7 Grand Wailea Resort Hotel & Spa

Opulent, lavish, deeply sumptuous – describing the Grand exhausts superlatives. The rooms are large and beautifully appointed, while dining choices include the sublime Kincha Japanese restaurant. But the jewel in the crown is the peerless Spa Grande. ✪ Wailea • Map E5 • 808 875 1234 • www.grandwailea.com • $$$$$

8 Four Seasons Resort at Wailea

Beyond the lovely grounds, excellent facilities, and comfortable rooms, you'll find one of chef Wolfgang Puck's celebrated Spago restaurants. The elegant spa features a minimalist, Zen-like environment. ✪ Wailea • Map E5 • 808 874 8000 • www.four seasons.com • $$$$$

9 The Fairmont Kea Lani Maui

Every guest suite (and they're all suites here) has a bedroom, large marble bath with a deep soaking tub, and a separate living room with a full entertainment system. A very good fish restaurant too. ✪ Wailea • Map E5 • 808 875 4100 • www.kealani. com • $$$$$

10 Hotel Hāna-Maui

No TVs, no radios, just one of the most beautiful and relaxing properties in Hawai'i. It's been updated with modern amenities and a spa, yet still retains its old Hawaiian flavor. ✪ Hāna • Map L4 • 808 248 8211 • www.hotel hanamaui.com • $$$$$

Note: Unless otherwise stated, all hotels accept credit cards, have full bathrooms, and air conditioning

Price Categories

For a standard,	**$** under $100
double room per	**$$** $100–$200
night (with breakfast	**$$$** $200–$300
if included), taxes,	**$$$$** $300–$400
and extra charges.	**$$$$$** over $400

Maui Marriott Resort & Ocean Club

TOP 10 Other Luxury Accommodations

Streetsmart

1 Maui Marriott Resort & Ocean Club

Following a major renovation, which included the creation of a "super-pool," the Marriott is an excellent choice for families. Set on world-famous Kā'anapali Beach, there are plenty of ocean activities steps away. Championship golf courses close by too. ✪ *100 Nohea Kai Dr., Kā'anapali • Map B2 • 808 667 1200 • www. marriott.com • $$$$*

2 Kā'anapali Ali'i

Because of its beachfront location, this condo complex is still the most fashionable condominium address in the area. The studio, one- and two-bedroom apartments are individually owned, so decors differ, but all units are well maintained and comfortable. No restaurants on site but plenty close by. ✪ *50 Nohea Kai Dr., Kā'anapali • Map B2 • 808 667 1400 • www. kaanapalialii.com • $$$$*

3 The Whaler on Kā'anapali Beach

Spacious accommodations, hotel-like services, and a perfect location smack in the middle of Kā'anapali Beach keep these older high-rises popular year after year. There's a small heated pool and five tennis courts on the property. ✪ *2481 Kā'anapali Parkway, Kā'anapali • Map B2 • 808 661 4861 • www.aston hotels.com • $$$$*

4 Kā'anapali Beach Hotel

Maui's most Hawaiian hotel, where the islands' values of *'ohana* (family) and *aloha* (love) abound. This is the only hotel in Hawai'i that serves authentic Hawaiian food. They also host great local acts. ✪ *2525 Kā'anapali Parkway, Kā'anapali • Map B2 • 808 661 0011 • www. kbhmaui.com • $$$*

5 Sands of Kahana

Set on a lovely beach halfway between Lahaina and the Kapalua resort, two distinctive high-rise buildings offer one-, two-, and three-bedroom apartments. Pool, Jacuzzi, tennis courts, barbecues, and a restaurant all on site. ✪ *4299 Honoapi'ilani Rd., Kahana • Map C2 • 808 669 0423 • www. sands-of-kahana.com • $$$*

6 Wailea Beach Marriott Resort and Spa

The resort has undergone a $60 million renovation. All the suites and guestrooms have been redesigned, as have all the restaurants, the fitness center, and the Mandara spa. ✪ *3700 Wailea Alanui, Wailea • Map E5 • 808 879 1922 • www.marriott. com • $$$*

7 Wailea Grand Champion Villas

These California-style condos are great for sporty types – the sprawling complex of low-rise buildings overlooks Wailea's golf and tennis facilities, and there are two pools on site. The accommodations are upscale and very comfortable. ✪ *155 Wailea Ike Pl., Wailea • Map E5 • 808 879 1595 • $$$$*

8 Maui Polo Beach Club

On a white sand beach at the Mākena end of the Wailea resort area, these accommodations are elaborately decorated and all have ocean views. ✪ *20 Mākena Rd., Mākena • Map E5 • 808 879 1595 • $$$$$*

9 Mākena Surf

The one-, two-, and three-bedroom apartments in this gated community are the most private and luxurious on Maui's south shore. The units are oceanfront, but the coastline here is more rocky than sandy. Two vast pools, Jacuzzis, and tennis courts complete the picture. ✪ *Map E5 • 808 879 1595 • $$$$$*

10 Maui Prince Hotel

A Garden of Eden-like atrium is at the heart of the stark white Maui Prince, the farthest afield of the south-side resorts. The beach here is fabulous: sun, shade, and perfect ocean conditions for the whole family. And the Sunday brunch is legendary. ✪ *5400 Makena Alanui, Wailea • Map E5 • 808 874 1111 • www.princeresorts hawaii.com • $$$$$*

Check out www.destinationresortshi.com for information about Wailea's Grand Champion Villas, Polo Beach Club, and Mākena Surf

Left **Nāpili Kai Beach Resort** Right **Hāna Kai-Maui Resort**

🔟 Mid-Price Hotels

1 Puamana
A series of low-rise apartments within walking distance of Lahaina but seemingly far from the hustle and bustle of town. There's a children's playground, a clubhouse for reading, relaxing, and table tennis, and a good beach. Minimum stay of five nights. ✪ *Lahaina • Map C3 • 808 661 3484 • www.whalersrealty.com • $$$$*

2 Outrigger Aina Nalu
If you're likely to spend most of your time in and around Lahaina, consider this 10-acre complex right in town. The apartments are located in a low-rise building that is surrounded by gardens. There's also a swimming pool. ✪ *660 Waine'e St., Lahaina • Map C3 • 808 667 7966 • www.outrigger.com • $$*

3 Kā'anapali Beach Club
Accommodation here consists of spacious two-room suites with a living room and private bedroom. The grounds feature waterfalls, a one-acre heated pool, and an 18-hole miniature golf course. ✪ *104 Ka'anapali Shores Place, Ka'anapali • Map B2 • 808 661 2000 • www.kaanapali-beach-club.com • $$$$*

4 Kā'anapali Shores
This beachfront condo is great for families. All studios and suites have fully equipped kitchens and some have washer-dryers. Amenities include a restaurant, a shop, two pools, tennis courts, and a children's program. ✪ *3445 Lower Honoapi'ilani Hwy. • Map B2 • 808 667 2211 • www.astonhotels.com • $$$$*

5 Kahana Sunset
A no-frills place, the secluded beach and laid-back style are the main assets. Closer to Nāpili than to Kahana, some of the varied accommodations are close to the water. There's a garden with a barbecue and a pool too. ✪ *4909 Lower Honoapi'ilani Hwy. • Map C2 • 808 669 8700, 1-800 669 1488 • www.kahana sunset.com • $$$*

6 Nāpili Kai Beach Resort
A truly charming resort, its location on a world-class beach is unparalleled on the island. Rooms are comfortable and you'll be treated like family. Staff here founded the Nāpili Kai Foundation to teach Hawaiian culture to Maui's children, and the kids put on a wonderful hula show on Tuesdays. ✪ *5900 Honoapi'ilani Rd. • Map C2 • 808 669 6271, 1-800 367 5030 • www.napilikai.com • $$$$*

7 Punahoa Beach Apartments
If you love falling asleep to the sound of the surf, this could be for you. Indeed, it's the main attraction at this small condo, which has little else by way of recreational facilities. But the views are spectacular. ✪ *2142 'Ili'ili Rd., Kīhei • Map E4 • 808 879 2720 • $$$*

8 Maui Coast Hotel
Across the street from several Kīhei beach parks, the rooms are clean and comfortable. There's a restaurant on site, as well as a pool, two whirlpool spas, two tennis courts, and laundry facilities. And you'll be within walking distance of lots of shops and restaurants. ✪ *2259 S. Kīhei Rd., Kīhei • Map E4 • 808 874 6284 • www.mauicoasthotel.com • $$*

9 Hale Hui Kai
A complex comprising a couple of dozen two-bedroom, two-bath units. And while not by any means fancy, they're right on the water fronting a wide, mile-long beach. Being on the fringe of Wailea, it's quiet too. ✪ *2994 S. Kīhei Rd., Kīhei • Map E4 • 808 879 1219 • www.halehuikai maui.com • $$$*

10 Hāna Kai-Maui Resort
"Basic" is the best word to describe the accommodations; "totally awesome" the way to sum up the site. The only condos in Hāna, they sit directly above the pounding surf. ✪ *1533 Uakea Rd., Hāna • Map L4 • 808 248 8426 • www.hanakai maui.com • $$$*

Note: *Unless otherwise stated, all hotels accept credit cards, have full bathrooms, and air conditioning*

Left **The Old Wailuku Inn at Ulupono** Right **Plantation Inn**

Inns, Cottages, & Guest Houses

Ho'oilo House
The breathtaking view of the Pacific can be enjoyed from just about everywhere in this quiet and luxurious B&B. The spacious suites each have a private *lanai* with an outdoor shower. Children are not allowed. ✆ *138 Awaiku St. Lahaina • Map C3 • 808 667 6669 • www. hooilohouse.com • $$$$*

Lahaina Inn
The nine rooms and three parlor suites in this lovely and well-located inn are decorated in Victorian style. Modern conveniences are mixed with antiques. Continental breakfast included. ✆ *127 Lahainaluna Rd., Lahaina • Map C3 • 808 661 0577 • www.lahainainn.com • $$*

Plantation Inn
This charming 19-room inn combines plantation-era style with 21st-century convenience. Tucked away in its own bubble of serenity, the inn has a Jacuzzi and pool open 24 hours. Breakfast (included) is prepared by Gerard's, a wonderful French restaurant that occupies the front of the building. ✆ *174 Lahainaluna Rd., Lahaina • Map C3 • 808 667 9225 • www. the plantationinn.com • $$$*

The Old Wailuku Inn at Ulupono
Janice and Tom Fairbanks have lovingly transformed their 1924 home into seven singular guestrooms, complete with Hawaiian quilts and some whirlpool tubs. Three rooms also feature standing spas. Full, and delicious, breakfast included. ✆ *2199 Kaho'okele St., Happy Valley, Wailuku • Map N2 • 808 244 5897 • www.mauiinn.com • $$*

Eva Villa
Located in Maui Meadows (an upscale residential area), all the rooms here have private baths and separate living rooms. There's a heated pool, a Jacuzzi, and fresh breakfast foods are left in the fridge each day. ✆ *815 Kumulani Dr., Kīhei • Map E4 • 808 874 6407 • $$*

Haiku Plantation Inn
Built in 1850 to attract a doctor to the area, this plantation-style home now welcomes guests to four nicely appointed rooms, all with private baths. Breakfast is served in the home's dining room or may be enjoyed in the tropical Upcountry air, amid lush vegetation. ✆ *555 Ha'ikū Rd., Ha'ikū • Map G2 • 808 298 6579 • www.haikuleana.net • $$*

Pā'ia Inn
It is amazingly quiet inside this stylish inn, despite the busy location in the heart of Pā'ia. Guests enter through a pleasant courtyard to the first-floor lobby and bedrooms are upstairs (note there is no elevator). Although they are small, the rooms are well appointed. ✆ *93 Hana Hwy., Pā'ia. • Map G2 • 808 579 6000 • $$$*

The Inn at Mama's Fish House
These nine units are located on a secluded beach. The one- and two-bedroom air-conditioned cottages are decorated in island-style and have full kitchens, televisions, laundry facilities, and gas barbecues. ✆ *799 Poho Pl., Kula • Map G2 • 579 9764 • $$$*

Kula Lodge
A good spot for a romantic getaway, this charming and cozy lodge is more like a mountain chalet than a tropical villa. Set high up on the slope of Haleakala, it offers expansive views of the ocean below. The grounds include a restaurant, an art gallery, and the Kula Marketplace. ✆ *15200 Haleakala Hwy., Kula • Map G4 • 808 878 1535 • www. kulalodge.com • $$$*

Hale Ho'okipa Inn
Listed on the State of Hawaii and National Historic Registrars, this charming and serene Craftsman-style house was built in 1924. It has been thoroughly restored and is comfortably furnished with period pieces. ✆ *32 Pakani Place, Makawao • Map G3 • 808 572 6698 • www.maui-bed-and-breakfast.com • $$*

Left **Pioneer Inn** Center **Banyan Tree House** Right **Camp Keʻanae**

Budget Accommodations

Pioneer Inn
The whaling ships and their rowdy crews may be gone, but the Pioneer Inn remains, right on Lahaina Harbor. These days, the 45 guest rooms are all air-conditioned (a must for hot Lahaina) and all have balconies. The bar and restaurant are popular. ✆ 658 Wharf St., Lahaina • Map C3 • 808 661 3636 • www.pioneerinnmaui.com • $$

Luana Kai
This condo is close to the beach and offers tennis courts, a putting green, and a pool area with a hot tub, saunas, and gas grills. Units have fully equipped kitchens and laundry facilities, and some have air-conditioning. ✆ 950 S. Kīhei Rd., Kīhei • Map E4 • 808 879 1268 • www.luanakai.com • $$

Banana Bungalow Maui Hostel
Dorm rooms, shared baths, communal kitchen, big garden, clean, comfortable, and safe, this is the place for the young, or youngish, backpacking and windsurfing set. Located in Central Maui, the hostel even offers free tours. ✆ 310 N. Market St., Wailuku • Map N1 • 808 244 5090 • www.mauihostel.com • $

Maui Ocean Breezes
Seemingly remote but only 10 minutes from Pāʻia and 15 minutes from the beach. The units have

fully equipped kitchens and there is a saltwater pool fed by a waterfall. No chemicals or pesticides are used on the property. ✆ 240 N. Holokai Rd., Haiku • Map H3 • 808 572 2775 • www.mauivacationhideway.com • $$

Banyan Tree House
Set among fabulous old plantation homes lining Baldwin Avenue, this property offers three rooms in its main house and four cottages. There's a formal dining room and living room and a well-equipped kitchen in the main house. ✆ 3265 Baldwin Ave., Makawao • Map G3 • 808 572 8482 • www.hawaii-mauirentals.com • $$

Camp Keʻanae
One of Maui's best-kept secrets. The location is absolutely fantastic: a cliff overlooking the Keʻanae Peninsula, where you can rent one of the attractive cabins or pitch a tent and use the communal bath facilities. ✆ 13375 Hāna Hwy., Keʻanae • Map J3 • 808 248 8355 • $

Hawaiʻi Division of State Parks
If you want to stay at the cabins or campgrounds at either Waiʻānapanapa or Polipoli Springs state parks, you'll need a permit from the government department for state parks. Waiʻānapanapa's 12 cabins are a great deal if you don't mind rustic accommodations – the

scenery is heavenly. There is only one cabin at Polipoli, so if you want to stay, you may have to plan your whole trip around its availability. ✆ Apply to: State of Hawaiʻi, Division of State Parks, 54 South High St. – Room 101, Wailuku • 808 984 8109 • $

Haleakalā National Park
No fee and no permit required to camp at Hosmer's Grove or Kīpahulu. But permits are required at Hōlua and Palikū. They are free and available at park headquarters on the day of your trip. Three cabins within the park are available by advance reservation at https://fnnp.org/wcr/. ✆ U.S. National Park Service, Haleakalā National Park, P.O. Box 369, Makawao • 808 572 4400 • www.nps.gov/hale • $

Hoʻokipa Haven Vacation Services
More than just accommodations, the folks at Hoʻokipa can help with activities, car rentals, even real estate if you decide to stay. Their vacation rentals range from budget to luxury; check their website for last-minute deals. ✆ 808 579 8282 • www.hookipa.com

Donna Chameleon
Donna can find you a place to stay to fit your budget and help with rental cars. ✆ 808 575 9933 • www.donnachameleon.com

Note: Full bathrooms and air conditioning are not included in the Budget Accommodations unless mentioned

Price Categories

For a standard, double room per night (with breakfast if included), taxes, and extra charges.

$	under $100
$$	$100–$200
$$$	$200–$300
$$$$	$300–$400
$$$$$	over $400

Left **Manele Bay Hotel** Right **Lodge at Ko'ele**

Moloka'i & Lāna'i Accommodations

Hotel Moloka'i
The only central hotel on the island. It's a local favorite because of its location, low rates, and fabulous Friday night entertainment. The accommodations are clean but very basic. Its Hula Shores restaurant is ocean-front and serves delicious breakfast, lunch, and dinner. ✆ Kaunakakai • Map C6 • 808 553 5347 • www.hotelmolokai.com • $$

Moloka'i Shores
A well-landscaped, low-rise condominium complex. The units are individually owned (as is the case pretty much throughout the island). For the most part, the decor is fine, often tropical in flavor, and the units are very well equipped. ✆ Kamehameha Hwy., Kaunakakai • Map C6 • 808 553 5954 • www.castle resorts.com • $$

Swenson Real Estate
This agency handles vacation rentals as well as real estate sales. So, if you'd like to rent a private home almost anywhere on the island, the folks at Swenson will be able to help. ✆ 808 553 3648

Paniolo Hale
This condominium complex on Moloka'i 's west side is an especially good choice for families. The variously sized units are individually owned but bookable through various reservation agencies. The complex is landscaped, and there's a swimming pool too. ✆ Maunaloa • Map A6 • 1 800 367 2984 • www.molokai-vacation-rental.com • $$

Dunbar Beach-front Cottages
These two plantation-style cottages, with their own secluded beach on Moloka'i's eastern end, offer privacy and great views of the Pacific and nearby islands. Each sleeps up to four, and has a fully-equipped kitchen and a large deck. Minimum three-night stay. Credit cards are not accepted. ✆ Kamehameha V Hwy. (at mile marker 18) • Map E1 • 808 558 8153 • www.molokai-beachfront-cottages.com • $$$

Ke Nani Kai
All the condos here have kitchens, balconies, and cable TV. Laundry facilities too, as well as barbecues, a putting green, tennis courts, and a swimming pool. ✆ Maunaloa • Map A6 • 1-800 367 2984 • $$

Four Seasons Resort Lāna'i, The Lodge at Kō'ele
Nestled among Cook pines and banyan trees, this secluded retreat is especially lauded for its service. Rooms and suites have four-poster beds and luscious feather pillows. The Great Room is grand indeed, with lots of nooks and crannies in which to relax with a good book. The dining is excellent, as are the recreational facilities. ✆ Ko'ele • Map L2 • 808 565 4000 • www.four seasons.com/lanai • $$$$$

Hotel Lāna'i
A lovely, refurbished 11-room hotel. Built in 1923, this historic building was originally a lodging for Dole Plantation executives. Today, it's home to Henry Clay's Rotisserie, an excellent choice of restaurant, regardless of where you stay. ✆ 828 Lana'i Ave. • Map L2 • 808 565 7211 • www.hotellanai.com • $$

Captain's Retreat
For a large family or group, this two-story home within walking distance of town is just the ticket. Four bedrooms (the master suite has its own bath and patio), a large deck surrounded by pines, an outdoor shower, and a big kitchen. Can accommodate eight. ✆ Lana'i City • Map L2 • 808 268 1834 • www.lanairental.com • $$$$$

Mānele Bay Hotel
This big, typical resort hotel will get you as close as you can get to the beach on Lāna'i. The rooms are large and luxurious, with marble baths and balconies. ✆ 1 Mānele Bay Rd. • Map L3 • 808 565 2000 • www.fourseasons.com/manele bay • $$$$$

General Index

Acknowledgments

The Author

Bonnie Friedman is a freelance writer and publicist based on Maui. She previously contributed to the DK Eyewitness Travel Guide to Hawai'i.

The author would like to thank Linda Mather Olds for her assistance while researching the guide.

Produced by
BLUE ISLAND PUBLISHING

Editorial Director Rosalyn Thiro
Art Director Stephen Bere
Associate Editor Michael Ellis
Picture Research Ellen Root
Proofreader Mary Sutherland
Indexer Jane Simmonds
Fact Checker Linda Mather Olds

Photographer Nigel Hicks
Additional Photography Phillip Dowell, Steve Gorton, David Murray, Ian O'Leary, Rob Reichenfeld, Mike Severns

Cartography

DK India: Managing Editor Aruna Ghose; Senior Cartographer Uma Bhattacharya; Cartographers Suresh Kumar and Alok Pathak

AT DORLING KINDERSLEY

Publisher Douglas Amrine
Publishing Manager Helen Townsend
Revisions Nicola Erdpresser; Anna Freiberger; Rhiannon Furbear; Laura Jones; Carly Madden; Sam Merrell; Mary Ormandy; Linda Mather Olds; Pure Content; Quadrum Solutions; Mani Ramaswamy; Susana Smith

Senior Art Editor Marisa Renzullo
Senior Cartographic Editor Casper Morris
Senior DTP Designer Jason Little
Production Controller Melanie Dowland

Picture Credits

Dorling Kindersley would like to thank all the churches, museums, hotels, restaurants, bars and other sights for their assistance and kind permission to photograph.

Placement Key
t=top; tl=top left; tr=top right; tc=top center; tcl=top center left; l=left; c=center; cr=center right; ca=center above; cb=center below; r=right; b=bottom; bl=bottom left; br=bottom right

BIEGEL COMMUNICATIONS INC: 52tr; RON DAHLQUIST: 30b, 32c, 33r, 34tr, 36tl/tr/c/b, 44c/b, 46c/b, 47, 63b 114tl; PETER FRENCH: 32tr courtesy of HAWAIIAN AIRLINES: 106tc; HOTEL LANA'I: 102tc; LEONARDO MEDIA LTD: 116tc; MAMA'S FISH HOUSE: Tony Clifford Novak 89tc; MAUI ARTS & CULTURAL CENTER: Tony Novak-Clifford 13clb; MAUI CRAFTS GUILD: 88tl; MOLOKA'I FERRY: 108tc; DOUGLAS PEEBELS: 26–7, 37br, 48c, 50tl/b, 53br; PINEAPPLE GRILL: Steve Brinkman Photography 69tl; Michael Nolan/ Wildlife Images 49bl; Darrell Wong 76–7; THE PLANTATION INN: 119C; ALAN SEIDEN: 30tl/tr, 31tr/br, 32tl, 35r

All other images © Dorling Kindersley. For further information see: www. dkimages.com

Glossary of Useful Words & Terms

Hawaiian began as an oral language and was put into written form by missionaries who arrived in the 1820s. The teaching and speaking of Hawaiian was banned from the early 1900s, and by the time the native cultural renaissance began in 1978 the melodious language was almost totally lost. Immersion programs are beginning to produce a new generation of Hawaiian speakers, however, and you will hear Hawaiian words sprinkled in conversation and in the islands' music, as well as seeing it written on some signs.

Summary of Pronunciation

The Hawaiian language has just 12 letters: the five vowels plus h, k, l, m, n, p, and w.

unstressed vowels:

a	as in "above"
e	as in "bet"
i	as y in "city"
o	as in "sole"
u	as in "full"

stressed vowels:

ā	as in "far"
ē	as in "pay"
ī	as in "see"
ō	as in "sole"
ū	as in "moon"

consonants:

h	as in "hat"
k	as in "kick"
l	as in "law"
m	as in "mow"
n	as in "now"
p	as in "pin"
w	as in "win" or "vine"

The 'okina (glottal stop) is found at the beginning of some words beginning with vowels or between vowels. It is pronounced like the sound between the syllables in the English "uh-oh."

ali'i	ahlee-ee
liliko'i	leeleekoh-ee
'ohana	oh-hahnah

The kahakō (macron) is a mark found only above vowels, indicating vowels should be stressed.

kāne	**kah**-nay
kōkua	**koh**-koo-ah
pūpū	**poo**-poo

Everyday Words

aloha	ah-loh-ha	hello; goodbye; love
hale	ha-leh	house
hula	who-la	Hawaiian dance
kāhiko	**kaa**-hee-koh	old, traditional
kapa	kah-pah	bark cloth
keiki	kay-kee	child
kōkua	**koh**-koo-ah	help
lānai	**luh**-nigh	porch; balcony
lei	layh	garland
lua	looah	bathroom
mahalo	muh-ha-low	thank you
'ono	oh-noh	delicious
ko'olau	koh-oh-lowh	windward side

Geographical & Nature Terms

'a'ā	ah-**aah**	rough, jagged lava
kai	kaee	ocean
koholā	koh-hoh-**laah**	humpback whale
mauna	mau-nah	mountain
pāhoehoe	**pah**-hoy-hoy	smooth lava
pali	pah-lee	cliff
pu'u	poo-oo	hill
wai	w(v)hy	fresh water

Historical Terms

ali'i	ahlee-ee	chief; royalty
heiau	hey-yowa	ncient temple
kahuna	kah-hoo-nah	priest; expert
kapu	kah-poo	taboo
kupuna	koo-poo-nah	elders; ancestors
luakini	looh-ah-kee-nee	human sacrifice temple
mana	mah-nah	supernatural power
mele	meh-leh	song
oli	oh-leeh	chant

Food Words

'ahi	ah-hee	yellowfin tuna
aku	ah-koo	skipjack; bonito
a'u	ah-oo	swordfish; marlin
haupia	how-peeah	coconut pudding
kalo	kah-loh	taro
kālua	**kah**-looah	food baked slowly in an underground oven
laulau	lau-lau	steamed filled ti-leaf packages
liliko'i	lee-lee-koh-ee	passion fruit
limu	lee-moo	seaweed
lomi-lomi salmon	low-me low-me	raw salmon with onion and tomato
lū'au	**loo**-ow	Hawaiian feast
mahimahi	muh-hee-muh-hee	dorado; dolphin fish
poi	poy	pounded taro
pūpū	**poo-poo**	appetizer
uku	oo-koo	gray snapper
ulua	oo-looah	jackfish

Pidgin

Hawai'i's unofficial conglomerate language is commonly heard on the street and in backyards throughout Hawai'i. You may hear:

brah	brother, pal
broke da mout'	great food
fo' real	really
fo' what	why
grinds	food; also to grind
howzit?	how's everything?
kay den	okay then
laydahs	later; goodbye
no can	cannot
no mo' nahting	nothing
shoots!	yeah!
stink eye	dirty look
talk story	chat; gossip